THE
BUSINESS
GRAMMAR
HANDBOOK

THE BUSINESS GRAMMAR HANDBOOK

Scott R. Pancoast and Lance M. White

M. EVANS AND COMPANY, INC.
New York

Library of Congress Cataloging-in-Publication Data

Pancoast, Scott R.
  The business grammar handbook.

  Includes index.
  1. English language—Business English—Handbooks,
manuals, etc.   2. English language—Rhetoric—Handbooks,
manuals, etc.   3. English language—Grammar—1950–
Handbooks, manuals, etc.   I. White, Lance M.   II. Title.
PE1479.B87P36   1986   428.2′02465   85-20248

ISBN 0-87131-488-6

M. Evans and Company, Inc.
216 East 49 Street
New York, New York 10017

Manufactured in the United States of America

9 8 7 6 5 4 3 2

This book is dedicated to our parents.

ACKNOWLEDGMENTS

Edward L. Hutton, CEO of Chemed Corporation and a sound grammarian, deserves much of the credit for this book. His grammar consciousness rubbed off on us when we were young, and his attention to communications detail planted the seeds for the writing of this book.

The kind people at M. Evans and Company, as well as, David Vigliano, assisted in the conceptual stages and in the editing functions. In the area of production, Wanda Luster, Jan Wrassman, and Barb Wiles all lent a helping hand, and Lillian Brueggemeyer and Lori Hunter each made an extra-special contribution. For the part played by each of these people, we are deeply grateful.

We consulted many reference books in writing *The Business Grammar Handbook*. The three that contributed most and that deserve special mention are: Theodore Bernstein's *The Careful Writer: A Modern Guide to English Usage* (published by Leonard Harris, New York, 1967); William Strunk, Jr., and E. B. White's *The Elements of Style* (the third edition was published by The Macmillan Company, New York, 1979); and *Webster's New World Dictionary of the American Language, Second College Edition* (published by William Collins & World Publishing Co., Inc., Cleveland, Ohio, 1976). If we were forced to reduce our reference library to only three volumes, these would be the three.

We also must thank Susan Lutz and Diane White for their support through this book-writing adventure.

CONTENTS

PREFACE *1*
HOW TO USE THIS BOOK *4*

I. GOOD GRAMMAR AT A GLANCE *5*

INTRODUCTION *7*

CHALLENGE AND REVIEW:
   1. Affect vs. Effect *10*
   2. Fewer Errors = Less Hassle *14*
   3. Percent vs. Percentage Point *16*
   4. Compare Notes *19*
   5. The Which Hunt *23*
   6. Sub-par Subjects *27*
   7. EPS Was/Were *30*
   8. To Be or Not To Be *32*
   9. Taboo or Not Taboo, Part I: Splitting
       Your Infinitives *36*
  10. Taboo or Not Taboo, Part II: Dangling Your
       Prepositions *39*
  11. Taboo or Not Taboo, Part III: And in
       the Beginning. *42*
  12. Subject/Verb Agreement, Part I: Noise *44*
  13. Subject/Verb Agreement, Part II: More Noise *47*
  14. Subject/Verb Agreement, Part III:
       Apportioning Nouns *50*
  15. Subject/Verb Agreement, Part IV:
       Singular Dollars *54*

16. Subject/Verb Agreement, Part V:
    Last but Not Least *56*
17. "Lastly" Is Least *59*
18. Numbers: Spell Out or Use Figures? *61*
19. Perilous Non-Parallels *65*
20. Give "Me" Some Respect *72*
21. "Myself" Misfits *76*
22. "The Data Is" . . . Incorrect! *79*
23. A Company: It or They? *82*
24. Be Real *84*
25. Placement, However, Is Difficult *87*
26. The Big IF *90*
27. Apostrophes: Possessing a Working Knowledge *92*
28. Commas, Commas, and More Commas *95*
29. The Semicolon: Big Brother of the Comma;
    Weak Sister of the Period *99*
30. Parenthetical Punctuation *102*
31. Hyphenate to Communicate *106*
32. The Magic Spell *110*
33. Relatively Redundant *112*
34. Passive vs. Active Voice *114*
35. Odds and (Year) Ends *117*
36. Credibility Checks *121*

II. GOOD GRAPHS AT A GLANCE

INTRODUCTION *127*

CHALLENGE AND REVIEW:
Introductory Challenge: Selection of a Chart Form *130*
1. The Important Cosmetics, Part I *142*
2. The Important Cosmetics, Part II *148*
3. Structure, Part I *154*
4. Structure, Part II *162*
5. Making the Calculation *171*
6. Footnotes *177*
7. Graphic Charts *182*
8. Summary *190*

APPENDIX A *192*
APPENDIX B *195*
APPENDIX C *196*

INDEX *197*

PREFACE

As everyday business writers who typically end up playing the role of editor, we have learned the importance of effective communication in the business world. Promising ideas (and promising careers) are oftentimes lost as a result of ineffective communication—ineffective communication involving words, data, or both. We have found that even the most highly educated of business writers have difficulty with certain grammar concepts and chart-presentation principles. In fact, it seems that most of us got through grade school grammar and never looked back. While we retained most of the basics, some of the more important principles have fallen through the cracks (of our memories) over the years. Regarding charts, it appears that most of us have had no guidance whatsoever on structure, presentation, or clarity; no school at any level provided much instruction in this area.

Despite the importance of communications in business, we have found no truly effective and readable business communications book on the market. The books available today that promise to teach grammar are, almost without exception, rehashes of grade school grammar—full of rules and their endless exceptions. In addition, these textbook-style books are too technical when it comes to the jargon used ("the predicate nominative in the participial phrase . . ."), too thin when it comes to communicating with numbers (few books even broach the topic of graphic presentation), and too thick when it comes to price (have you bought one of these books lately?). And, to top it all off, none of these books are written specifically *for* the business person *by* the business person.

As a result of this situation, we decided that a different, refreshing approach to business communications was needed. Hence, our book, *The Business Grammar Handbook*. This book does not attempt to address every rule of grammar and every exception; rather, it addresses—in a simple-to-understand style and a simple-to-learn format—only the most troublesome of problems. In other words, what we're going to teach you here is a simplified approach to coming up with the proper grammar and the effective chart without any grade school rote. In order to develop such an approach, we've done something different... and important. We have screened literally thousands of business documents and have made files of the many examples of poor grammar, ambiguous phrasing, and convoluted syntax we stumbled across. No business document (or conversation) was sacred— board rooms, annual reports, contracts, simple memos (both internal and intercompany), and even washroom conversations were fair game. After completing the filing phase, we categorized the errors and tallied them to determine which occurred most often. We gave heavy weight, in this tallying process, to errors occurring in annual reports (and, we might add, no annual report we've read has been error-free). There are two reasons we chose to do this. First, the tone in an annual report is typically formal, so no "we were being informal" excuses fly. Second, at least twenty professionals usually review an annual report before it goes to print—if an error escapes all twenty, it deserves heavy weight.

Tallying process completed, we discovered something quite interesting—a 90:10 rule, similar to the familiar 80:20 business rule (Pareto's law), seemed to apply to business-communications problems. That is, it appeared that ten percent of all communications rules were causing ninety percent of the problems. Marketing personnel, stockbrokers, general managers, accountants, and every other business type were all having problems "obeying" the same ten percent of business-related communications rules. It is these ten percent that our book focuses on.

Master the forty or so guidelines we provide, and you will eliminate ninety percent of your potential for significant grammar- and chart-related errors (and, hopefully, that little bit you remembered from grade school will take care of the other ten percent).

We have made an effort in this book to ensure that learning these forty or so guidelines will be easy to do. We walk you through each lesson, providing you with simple-to-read, simple-to-remember instructions without the use of technical grammar/communications jargon. We never tell you, for example, that a "gerund or verbal noun, when qualified, must be preceded by an adjective," as quoted from another communications book. Instead, we use language for the everyday business writer.

In addition, we have used the tried-and-true "challenge-then-review" technique throughout the book. At the beginning of each lesson, there is a quiz—termed "Challenge" in the book—in which the reader is asked to make appropriate corrections and improvements. Following each Challenge is a Review, consisting of an easy-to-understand explanation of the concept(s) involved as well as the answers to the Challenge. This challenge-then-review format allows you to involve yourself in the book.

And, in order to make the guidelines even easier to learn, we have divided the book into two sections. The first section, "Good Grammar at a Glance," is about communicating effectively with *words*; this section covers grammar, punctuation, structure, and writing strategy and represents a refreshing approach to solving the everyday business writer's everyday writing problems. The second section, "Good Graphs at a Glance," provides an insightful set of guidelines—never before offered—for communicating effectively with *numbers*; this section covers the effective presentation of graphs, charts, and illustrations. We feel this section of the book is especially relevant in today's business world, where everyone with access to a personal computer is capable of producing a chart with the touch of a finger; this situation has elevated the importance of chart presentation to new heights.

HOW TO USE
THIS BOOK

This book is *not* a reference book (reference books are not really read, only referred to). Your success with *The Business Grammar Handbook* depends on your reading and *enjoying* it. After reading it through and gaining an understanding of the various lessons, you can then use it for reference as necessary.

I
GOOD GRAMMAR AT A GLANCE

INTRODUCTION

Grammar, in general, means "a body of rules for speaking and writing a given language." "Good Grammar at a Glance," the first section of this book, is about *business* grammar, the body of rules for speaking and writing the *business* language. Business grammar is no different from "English" grammar; it is just more specialized. Business people have special demands, special needs, and special difficulties when it comes to communicating. Thus, a special body of rules facilitating the use of language is appropriate for the business person.

The problem with grammar for business is the problem that exists with any body of rules—no one can remember all of them. The "Good Grammar at a Glance" section of this book attempts to translate a huge body of rules (including all the exceptions to the rules) into a relevant, focused, and usable set of guidelines.

THE GUIDELINES

"I am a man of fixed and unbending principles, the first of which is to be flexible at all times."
   —*the late Senator Everett McKinley Dirksen*

Laying down any guidelines of grammar—be it English or business grammar—is difficult because several levels of usage exist. The hierarchy starts with the more formal levels at the top and relaxes with each stage, ending with the informal, colloquial level at the bottom. Generally, we have remained loyal to the more formal levels of usage in this book, primarily because most business correspondence, as well as most business presentations and speeches, is formal in tone. This formal level of usage is also the purest; it is the most conducive to concise, precise, and powerful communication. We realize, however, that in some cases the formal (or technically correct) language may be too pretentious or stilted for the typical business audience. We are careful to point out such instances in the book and to recommend alternative solutions. But remember, the formal level of usage is never "wrong" and is always a valuable tool.

To provide a sound basis for this "Good Grammar at a Glance" section, we sought guidance from many sources:

- The practices of outstanding writers, especially those in *The Wall Street Journal, Time* magazine, and *The New York Times.*
- Our observation of writing practices that promote clarity and quality of voice in communications.
- The opinions of authors of other grammar books.
- The personal preferences of the authors (our experience as real-world, business-document "editors" allows us some leeway in formulating "official" guidelines of the business language).

ORGANIZATION OF GUIDELINES

As stated in the preface, this book uses the challenge-then-review format. The statements in the Challenge sections are grouped according to the type of error that occurs in each statement—the title of the lesson is typically a hint as to what type of error to look for. In addition, the real-world examples that contain those real-world errors are attributed in this book to their real-world authors. We weren't shy when the authors were corporations (annual reports, brochures, etc.). But, to avoid embarrassing individuals and to maintain confidentiality in certain circumstances, we have left out most names and included instead only a title and an indication of company size. (Also, the excerpts themselves are sometimes revised, responsibly, to eliminate extraneous or confidential material.)

The mix of sources included in this book is primarily a function of our personal business agendas, so do not conclude that those given credit for error-filled excerpts are any less grammar-proficient than those whose errors do not appear in the book. In particular, two sources of grammar errors quoted in this section—J. Peter Grace, Jr., and *The Wall Street Journal*—are, considering their prolific output, remarkably error-free and effective communicators.

Affect vs. Effect

Challenge A
Lifestyle factors are expected to have an affect on certain segments of the health care market.

> Richardson-Vicks 1984 annual report

Challenge B
U.S. dollar comparisons have been effected unfavorably by the deterioration in the Canadian dollar.

> Report to the president of a $200-million-plus corporation

Challenge C
He also found time, through the Business Roundtable, to speak for the social responsibility of business with an eloquence and effect not seen before or since. He is arguably the only CEO of GE to deserve to stand in Valhalla alongside her legendary engineers and scientists.

> William M. Stanger of Summit, New Jersey, in a letter to the editor
> *The Wall Street Journal*, October 21, 1984

Make the appropriate corrections and read Review 1 to see how you did.

Affect vs. Effect

Considering that this is a book written *by* business persons *for* business persons, it would be a sin of omission if we failed to include a matrix. So, if you will excuse us, we present the humble 2 × 2 matrix on the following page, which should shed light on the ever-present "affect vs. effect" problem.

As highlighted in the chart on page 12, "effect" is used as a verb only occasionally, and "affect" is rarely used as a noun. Thus, this is a case where a when-in-doubt rule (such rules will be used throughout the book) comes in handy: *Use "effect" when you need a noun and use "affect" when you need a verb.*

The answers to Challenges A and B are shown in the matrix but are repeated below in case you overlooked them. Also shown below is the answer to Challenge C.

[A] Correct
Lifestyle factors are expected to have an *effect* on certain segments of the health care market.

[B] Correct
U.S. dollar comparisons have been *affected* unfavorably . . .

Challenge C is an interesting example because it actually could be interpreted two different ways:

[C] Correct [No correction needed.]
He . . . found time . . . to speak . . . with an eloquence and effect not seen before or since.

As in "with an effect *on the audience* not seen before or since."

	Used as a Noun		**Used as a Verb**	
Effect	definition:	An effect of something is its result or consequence.	definition:	To effect is to bring about.
	example:	Lifestyle factors are expected to have an *effect* on . . . the health care market.	example:	She effected much change when she took over the unit.
	How often used as a noun:	**very often**	How often used as a verb:	occasionally
Affect	definition:	An affect is a technical word for emotion or feeling.	definition:	To affect is to influence.
	example:	The manager was moved with affect when his secretary retired.	example:	U.S. dollar comparisons have been *affected* unfavorably by the deterioration . . .
	How often used as a noun:	very rarely	How often used as a verb:	**very often**

Also Correct

He . . . found time . . . to speak with an eloquence and *affect* not seen before or since.

As in "with an *emotion* not seen before or since."

Since Mr. Stanger appears from his letter to be an intelligent man, we will assume that he was, indeed, writing of his subject's *effect* and not his *affect*.

Fewer Errors = Less Hassle

Challenge A
Flexible Computer Corp. anticipates that most end users will require less than 20 modules.

> *Venture Magazine,* December 1984

Challenge B
Pete Rose broke Stan Musial's National League record with his 726th career double, 73 less than Tris Speaker's major league mark.

> *Cincinnati Post,* October 1, 1984

Challenge C
Less than $125,000 of the $415,000 receivable was collected from them.

> Credit manager of a regional distribution company

Make the appropriate corrections and read Review 2 to see how you did.

Fewer Errors = Less Hassle

"Fewer eggs, less sugar": a corny yet enlightening phrase that gives insight into the "fewer vs. less" decision. The guidelines to use when making such a decision are discussed below.

Any noun that is plural should take "fewer" (note Challenges A and B below).

[A] *Correct*
Flexible Computer Corp. anticipates that most end users will require *fewer* than 20 modules.

"Fewer" is used because "modules" is plural.

[B] *Correct*
Pete Rose broke Stan Musial's National League record with his 726th career double, 73 *fewer* [doubles] than Tris Speaker's major league mark.

"Fewer" is used because it refers to the plural "doubles."

"Less" should be used only with those nouns considered singular or those nouns referring to a single *sum* or *amount*.

Challenge C provides an interesting example: Is $125,000 in this instance considered singular or plural? As discussed in Review 15, dollar figures are almost always considered singular, since it is the *sum* of money that is being referred to rather than the individual dollars.

[C] *Correct [No correction needed.]*
Less than $125,000 of the $415,000 receivable was collected from them.

Percent vs. Percentage Point

Challenge A
Return on average shareholders' equity was 16.2% in 1980 and was 13.8% in 1979—a difference of 2.4%.

> H. B. Fuller 1983 annual report
> (As "read" from a table)

Challenge B
The prime rate decreased 0.75% last month (from 11.0% to 10.25%).

> Marketing manager of a gigantic data processing concern

Challenge C
The inflation rate increased 8.0% last year. [No additional information given.]

> Well-known economist

Make the appropriate corrections and read Review 3 to see how you did.

Percent vs. Percentage Point

A *percent* variance and a *percentage-point* variance are NOT the same thing. A percent variance involves *dividing things* (usually dollar amounts, population figures, or numbers of items). For example, if sales increase from $80 to $88, we divide $8 ($88 − $80) by $80 to get a ten percent (or 10%) increase. While not common, it is possible—and sometimes meaningful—to calculate the percent variance between two percent figures. If, for instance, return on investment increases from 10% to 12%, the percent increase is 20% ([12% − 10%]/10%). A percentage-point variance, on the other hand, *always* involves percent figures (rather than dollar amounts, population figures, or numbers of items) and is calculated by simply adding or subtracting. For example, going back to the return-on-investment scenario used above, the percentage-point increase would be 12% *minus* 10%, or two percentage points (or 2% pts.). Note that when return on investment increases from 10% to 12%, the percent increase is *20%* while the percentage-point increase is *2%* pts.

The discussion above is summarized in the matrix on the following page.

When using either of these terms, the important thing is to be clear. Provide enough of the facts so that the risk of confusing the reader is minimized.

Let's now review the Challenge statements.

[A] Correct
Return on average shareholders' equity was 16.2% in 1980 and was 13.8% in 1979—a difference of 2.4% *pts.*

	Percent Variance	Percentage Pt. Variance
Non-Percent Figures example: year 1 year 2 sales $80 $88	$$\frac{\$88-\$80}{\$80}=10\%\text{ variance}$$	NOT APPLICABLE
Percent Figures example: year 1 year 2 ROI 10% 12%	$$\frac{12\%-10\%}{10\%}=20\%\text{ variance}$$	$12\%-10\% = 2\%$ pt. variance

[B] Correct
The prime rate decreased 0.75% *pts.* last month . . .

Challenge C is not necessarily incorrect, for if the inflation rate increased from, say, 10.0% to 10.8%, then the rate really did increase 8.0%. The fault with Challenge C lies in the fact that the reader cannot readily determine, without additional information, what the economist means to say. Without this additional information, the reader may think that inflation increased 8.0% *pts.* from, say, a 10.8% rate to an 18.8% rate.

[C] Comment
Not necessarily incorrect; sentence needs clarification.

Compare Notes

Challenge A
When comparing this year's earnings to last year's, we are up X%.

> Commonly spoken and written

Challenge B
Each pilot, navigator, or other member of an air crew is required to spend more than two weeks at the school here near Spokane, learning the rigors of wilderness living—and also getting a graphic demonstration that wilderness life is cozy compared to the horrors endured by a downed flier who is captured and made a prisoner of war.

> Gerald F. Seib, "Avoid the Hemlock, Savor the Porcupine, Drink Lots of Water"
> *The Wall Street Journal,* August 3, 1984

Challenge C
In a year when the steel industry continued to operate at diminished levels compared to several years ago, Quaker achieved record sales in real terms.

> Quaker Corporation 1983 annual report

Challenge D

The man in front of me, who had driven down from Missoula, Montana, thought the auction was a national tragedy, and, by way of illustration, compared it to some recent domestic misfortune of his own.

> Alexander Cockburn, "A Chapter of Our History Is Being Shredded"
> *The Wall Street Journal,* October 4, 1984

Make the appropriate corrections and read Review 4 to see how you did.

Compare Notes

"Compare *to*" or "compare *with*"? If you know the difference, then I would compare you *to* Daniel Webster (of dictionary fame). If you do not, then you are not too bad off, at least compared *with* most business persons.

The easiest way to deal with the potential confusion between "compare to" and "compare with" is to remember our when-in-doubt rule: *Use "compare* with" *in almost all everyday business uses*.

Alternatively, you can try to remember the technicalities, listed below:

1. Use "compare *with*" when you are placing two things side by side to observe or discover similarities or differences:

[A] Correct
... comparing this year's earnings *with* last year's ...

[B] Correct
... wilderness life is cozy compared *with* the horrors endured by a downed flier ...

[C] Correct
... operate at diminished levels compared *with* several years ago ...

2. Use "compare *to*" only when your purpose is to liken two things or to regard them as similar:

[D] Correct [No correction needed.]
The man in front ... compared [the auction] to some recent domestic misfortune of his own.

The author is indeed correct in this case, for the man *likened* the auction—"a national tragedy"—*to* a "recent domestic misfortune of his own."

Since "compare to" is typically used when speaking in a figurative context, whereas "compare with" is appropriate in almost all business-related contexts, we would advise that you get used to saying "compare *with*."

The same rules apply to "comparison with to" and "comparable with to."

The Which Hunt

Challenge A
We . . . oppose any attempts to increase taxes which would harm the recovery . . .

> Early draft, 1984 Republican Party policy platform

Challenge B
Specialty gases are included in this section because they are also used by the same end users which buy the inorganic materials.

> Strategic Analysis, Inc.

Challenge C
Included were general ledger, accounts receivable, accounts payable, and fixed-assets accounting packages, plus a tutorial which helps users learn basic data input procedures.

> American Brands, Inc., 1983 annual report

Make the appropriate corrections and read Review 5 to see how you did.

The Which Hunt

Contrary to popular belief, the words "that" and "which" are not interchangeable. Beginning a clause with the word "that" communicates a meaning different (in some cases, very different) from that of the same clause beginning with the word "which."

Let's use Challenge A as an example, for it is real-world proof that careless use of either of these words can create a great deal of confusion. As Challenge A now stands, the word "which" is used, but it is used carelessly (we'll discuss why below). As a result of this carelessness, the sentence can be interpreted to mean one of two things: (1) that the Republican Party opposes only those tax increases that would be harmful to the recovery (but *not* those that would be neutral or helpful) or (2) that the Republican Party opposes any and all tax increases (because *any* tax increase, according to this interpretation, would be harmful to the recovery). In other words, one interpretation leaves the door open for a tax increase while the other has slammed it shut—a big difference in these big-deficit days.

To gain insight into why the above equivocation exists, we must examine the overall differences between "that" and "which." Note the two sentences below.

I am searching for the lawn mower *that* is red.
I am searching for the lawn mower, *which* is red.

In the first example, there exist several lawn mowers in the author's universe, but the "that" clause provides *necessary* information that limits our search to a single mower—the one that is red. In the second example, there is only one mower to begin with; the "which" clause simply provides additional, *but not necessary,* information—that this one mower just happens to be red. Catch the difference? A "that" clause provides *necessary* information; without it, the reader is uncertain which particular thing, object, or idea you are talking about. A "which" clause, on the other hand, provides *unnecessary* (although sometimes interesting) information; without it, the reader would still know which particular thing, object, or idea you are talking about.

Another primary difference between "that" and "which" should be evident from the two examples used above. A "which" clause should always be preceded by a comma (or a parenthesis or a dash) while a "that" clause never needs such an accompaniment. This primary difference is the basis for our "which vs. that" when-in-doubt rule, which reads as follows:

Use "that" unless the clause in question can be treated as a parenthetical-type clause (i.e., can be left out of the sentence altogether without materially changing the meaning of the sentence). In the case of parenthetical-type clauses, use "which" (and use some form of punctuation, usually a comma, to set off the clause).

Let's now review the Challenge statements.

Challenge A is ambiguous because there is no comma before the word "which." Without a comma, the "which" can be interpreted to mean "that"—thus the confusion. So, depending on the intention of the Republican Party, the following statements are correct.

If the party opposes any and all tax increases:

[A] Correct
We . . . oppose any attempts to increase taxes, which would harm the recovery . . .

If the party opposes only harmful taxes:

[A] Correct
We . . . oppose any attempts to increase taxes *that* would harm the recovery . . .

The "which" in Challenge B should be a "that" because the clause at the end of the sentence is necessary information—it limits the universe of end users to those who buy the inorganic materials.

[B] Correct
Specialty gases are included in this section because they are also used by the same end users *that* buy the inorganic materials.

The "which" in Challenge C should also be a "that." The ending clause does not simply provide additional information. Rather, it provides information necessary to the identification of the tutorial. American Brands is not talking about tutorials in general, but about the type "that helps users learn basic data input procedures."

[C] Correct
Included were general ledger, accounts receivable, accounts payable, and fixed-assets accounting packages, plus a tutorial that helps users learn basic data input procedures.

Sub-par Subjects

Challenge A
Earnings per share of $11.84 were ... a record.

> General Motors 1983 annual
> report

Challenge B
Compensation, adjusted for these expenses, is shown in the following table.

> CEO and president of a large
> regional company

Challenge C
Even so, GM's best-ever overseas retail sales in 1983 are a demonstration of our ability to compete outside North America in today's economic climate.

> General Motors 1983 annual
> report

Make the appropriate corrections and read Review 6 to see how you did.

Sub-par Subjects

Be careful when using "earnings," "earnings per share," "compensation," "sales," "productivity," "income," and similar dollar-related words as subjects of sentences. As a subject, this type of word can sometimes make a sentence sound awkward or distorted. To illustrate, let's look at Challenge A. Do you think it is precise to say "earnings were a record"? Or would it be more precise (and smoother) to say "the earnings figure was a record"? Earnings do not become a record—the word "earnings" is too general in nature. But an earnings *figure* does become a record. We would strongly recommend, therefore, the following passage over GM's version in Challenge A.

[A] Strongly Recommended
The earnings-per-share *figure* of $11.84 was . . . a record.

Let's now review the other Challenge statements.

Take a good look at Challenge B. Is compensation shown in a table or are compensation *data* shown? As Challenge B is written, you would almost expect a few dollar bills or a company check—forms of compensation—to be shown in the chart that follows. To eliminate the curious ring of Challenge B, we recommend the following alternatives.

[B] Strongly Recommended
Compensation data . . . are shown in the following table.

or
Compensation levels from 19____ . . . are shown in the following table.

As for Challenge C, would you ever say "our best-ever sales are $1 billion"? Or would you alternatively phrase it as: "our

28 **THE BUSINESS GRAMMAR HANDBOOK**

best-ever sales *level* was $1 billion"? The phrase "best-ever sales" used as a subject is awkward at best and often misleading. Our recommended alternatives are as follows:

[C] Strongly Recommended

...GM's best-ever overseas retail sales performance [or level]...is a demonstration...

or

...GM's best-ever performance in the overseas retail market is a demonstration...

or

...GM's record level of overseas retail sales is a demonstration...

To be sure, there are situations in which the type of word discussed above does not refer to a specific number or figure. In such cases, using these words as the subject of a sentence is appropriate. The following excerpt from General Motors' annual report is a good example.

> Sales of GM's new mid-engine, two-passenger Pontiac Fiero were so rapid that dealers were unable to keep up with demand.

EPS Was/Were

Challenge A
EPS was up X% last year.

>   A common sentence

Challenge B
EPS were up X% last year.

>   A common sentence

Make the appropriate corrections and read Review 7 to see how you did.

EPS Was/Were

Some say "EPS" is plural because it stands for the *plural* noun phrase, "earning*s* per share."

Some say "EPS" is singular because abbreviations seem to be singular in nature (and besides, saying "EPS were" sounds funny).

We see logic on both sides of the fence but feel that neither logic is overwhelming. Technically, we would side with "EPS were." But we think that both "EPS were" *and* "EPS was" sound funny. Consequently, our recommendation is to avoid making such a decision altogether. Instead, restructure the phrase by saying "The EPS figure was up...," "The EPS figure of $____ was up...," or "We increased EPS by ____%..." Alternatively, simply avoid abbreviating the phrase: "Earnings per share were up..."

[A], [B] Comment
Suggest restructuring both sentences.

To Be or Not To Be

Challenge A
If anyone should be confused at this point, it should be I.

> Memo from E. L. Hutton, president and CEO of Chemed Corporation, to J. Peter Grace, chairman of W. R. Grace & Co. and chairman of Chemed Corporation

Challenge B
If anyone should be excited at this point, it should be I.

> Excerpt from a speech delivered by a new plant manager to all the plant employees during a company picnic

Make the appropriate corrections and read Review 8 to see how you did.

To Be or Not To Be

R-r-r-r-ring.
"Hello?"
"May I speak to Garth, please?"
"This is he..."

"This is (s)he." ... It seems we all have learned that such a statement is correct on the telephone. But what about in communications beyond the telephone? Should not this statement (and ones like it) also be correct then? The answer is yes, but apparently most business people either aren't aware of it or refuse to believe it, for we have searched day and night, through thick conversation and thin, and have come across very few of the following type of phrase (which happens to be correct):

It was he
If I were she

and quite a handful of this type (which is incorrect):

It was him
If I were her

Because of this lack of follow-through (from phone conversations to written and spoken communications), we feel a run-through of this lesson is necessary.

The verb "to be" has many conjugations: am, was, has been, had been, will be, is, were, have been, are, etc. Each of these conjugations of "to be" is an equalizer: It equates what precedes it with what follows it:

1. The truck is red $\Rrightarrow$ truck = red
2. The company will be bankrupt $\Rrightarrow$ company = bankrupt
3. It was he $\Rrightarrow$ It = he

And, since we all know that when a is equal to b, b must be equal to a, we can test the above sentences by reversing the statements. Such a "reversal" is shown below for each of the three sentences.

1. Red is the truck.
2. Bankrupt will be the company.
3. He was it.

Each of the sentences still sounds correct, even when "reversed." This means the "un-reversed" sentences are correct.

Let's now examine sentence number 3 above more closely. As mentioned earlier, we have found that most people tend to say "It was him" (rather than "It was he"). By testing this "popular" version, however, we end up with "Him was it," which is obviously wrong. The same applies to "If I were her." By testing, we get "If her were I," again incorrect.

We have just shown above that saying "It was him" is technically incorrect. We have also shown, on the other hand, that saying "It was he" is correct, at least technically. But we hasten to qualify any implied endorsement of the latter phrasing, for saying such things as "It was he" sounds pompous to certain people. We would recommend that these "technically correct" phrases be used only in formal situations. In other situations, to avoid the technically correct phrases, we recommend one of these three alternatives: (1) Alter the structure of the phrase altogether ("He was it" or "He was the one"); (2) Use an actual name rather than a pronoun ("It was Garth"); or (3) Take a chance and be technically incorrect (recommended only in the most informal of situations and only for the adventurous individual). Now for the Challenge statements.

Challenges A and B are essentially identical and both are technically correct. We would contend, however, that while

Challenge A is appropriate, Challenge B is not. Challenge A is an excerpt from a formal memorandum from one top-level (and "grammar-conscious") executive to another. Challenge B, on the other hand, is excerpted from an informal speech delivered in an informal setting. The new plant manager who delivers the speech wants to "fit in" as much as possible with his subordinates. Therefore, just as he shouldn't wear his pheasant-speckled cords and pink polo shirt to the picnic, so he shouldn't say "...it should be I." We recommend, instead, that the plant manager say: "If anyone should be excited at this point, *I* should."

[A] *Correct [No correction needed.]*
If anyone should be confused at this point, it should be I.

[B] *Preferred*
If anyone should be excited at this point, *I* should.

Taboo or Not Taboo,
Part I: Splitting Your Infinitives

Challenge A
Our company's objective is to skillfully develop selected properties.
A new-venture business plan

Challenge B
The chart is presented to further justify the expenditure.
Request for capital appropriation, W. R. Grace & Co.

Challenge C
Earnings are expected to more than triple next year.
Investment analyst

Make the appropriate corrections and read Review 9 to see how you did.

Taboo or Not Taboo,
Part I: Splitting Your Infinitives

These are infinitives:

> to have
> to behold
> to love
> to cherish

These are infinitives that have been split:

> to humbly have
> to further behold
> to almost love
> to more than cherish

Splitting infinitives is a sin only in the minds of hair-splitting grammarians (and their many disciples). While we believe that splitting an infinitive is generally to be avoided (it can muddy the meaning of a sentence), there are certain cases in which splitting an infinitive is not only possible, but actually preferred. The following list describes three such cases. (Note that each of the three cases uses one of the Challenge statements as an example.)

When splitting an infinitive avoids confusion. If we were to "de-split" Challenge A, we would end up with "Our company's objective is to develop skillfully selected properties." Does "skillfully" modify "develop" or "selected"? Because such ambiguity is eliminated by splitting the infinitive, we regard Challenge A as correct.

[A] Comment
Acceptable as written.

When splitting an infinitive avoids an awkward construction.
The "de-split" version of Challenge B—"This chart is presented
to justify further the expenditure"—is awkward. We like the
original version of Challenge B.

[B] Comment
Acceptable as written.

When splitting an infinitive is "unavoidable." Just try to
"de-split" Challenge C. We dare you.

[C] Comment
Acceptable as written.

The caveat in splitting your infinitives: Contained in your
audience may be those who are disciples of the hair-splitting
grammarians. So, before you split an infinitive, be certain that
you have shown infinite wisdom in your infinitive split.

Taboo or Not Taboo,
Part II: Dangling Your Prepositions

Challenge A
Education . . . is something the son of immigrants can believe in.

> Lawrence Minard, "A Boy Scout
> in Lotusland"
> *Forbes,* February 27, 1984

Challenge B
The reviewer did not have the foggiest idea what it was all about.

> Herbert Stein, "Help Wanted:
> President, Must Have . . ."
> *The Wall Street Journal,* August
> 14, 1979

Challenge C
No investor can possibly forecast what he will be investing in.

> J. Peter Grace, chairman of
> W. R. Grace & Co., and chair-
> man of Chemed Corporation,
> in a memorandum to E. L.
> Hutton, CEO and president of
> Chemed Corporation

Make the appropriate corrections and read Review 10 to see how you did.

Taboo or Not Taboo,
Part II: Dangling Your Prepositions

A dangling preposition is a preposition ("at," "to," "by," "with," "on," "in," "about," "of"...) that appears at the end of a sentence. There is nothing wrong with dangling prepositions, despite the decades-long conspiracy against such a practice. The conspiracy got its start, we believe, because some sentences ending with a preposition are awkward, and unnecessary. For example:

Awkward, Unnecessary	Recommended Version
Where is he at?	Where is he?
Where are they going to?	Where are they going?
What is she doing that for?	Why is she doing that?

The phrases on the left all end with a preposition, and all are to be avoided (especially the first, which should make any self-respecting communicator cringe). On the other hand, let's take a look at some sentences ending with prepositions that are considered idiomatic.

What is this world coming to?
That man can't be dealt with.
What is this book about?
This is the stuff that real business writers are made of.
I'm tough to buy presents for.

Surely, not even a determined conspirator could find anything wrong with these. These expressions have become idiomatic—and thus well accepted—over time because the alternative means of structuring the expressions either are awkward or sound pompous:

To what is this world coming?
That man is one with whom we can't deal.
About what is this book?
This is the stuff of which real business writers are made.
I'm one for whom it's tough to buy presents.

Similarly, there exist many other expressions ending in prepositions that are not necessarily idiomatic but that are certainly acceptable because the alternative structurings are awkward or stuffy. The three Challenge statements represent good examples.

[A] Preferred
Education . . . is something the son of immigrants can believe in.

Alternative, less desirable structuring (No Oomph)
Education . . . is something in which the son of immigrants can believe.

[B] Preferred
The reviewer did not have the foggiest idea what it was all about.

Alternative, less desirable structuring (Awkward)
The reviewer did not have the foggiest idea about what it all was.

[C] Preferred
No investor can possibly forecast what he will be investing in.

Alternative, less desirable structuring (Stuffy)
No investor can possibly forecast in what he will be investing.

As a final point, we will leave you with this when-in-doubt rule: *Unless the dangling construction is a weak one, leave it be.*

Taboo or Not Taboo,
Part III: And in the Beginning...

Challenge A

Four score and seven years ago our fathers brought forth on this continent, a new nation, conceived in Liberty, and dedicated to the proposition that all men are created equal.

Now we are engaged in a great civil war, testing whether that nation, or any nation so conceived and so dedicated, can long endure. We are met on a great battle-field of that war. We have come to dedicate a portion of that field, as a final resting place for those who here gave their lives that that nation might live. It is altogether fitting and proper that we should do this.

But, in a larger sense, we can not dedicate—we can not consecrate—we can not hallow...

President Abraham Lincoln,
Gettysburg Address

Challenge B

Most of the credit programs have been created for good reason. But they have gotten out of hand.

Stephen Berger, ''The Dangers
of Off-Budget Antics''
The New York Times, September 2, 1984

Make the appropriate corrections and read Review 11 to see how you did.

Taboo or Not Taboo,
Part III: And in the Beginning...

Although your old schoolmarm may have strictly forbade starting a sentence with "and," "but," or "or," such a practice is allowable. But do proceed with caution, for sometimes the practice will result in choppy, unrhythmic sentence flow.

We have found few pieces of writing that are better written and more cohesive than Lincoln's Gettysburg Address. The use of "but" to begin a sentence in the document is no exception; its meaning is clear and its placement effective. We decided to use example A for those who are not yet fully convinced that starting a sentence with "and," "but," or "or" is acceptable.

[A] Comment
Acceptable as written.

We have taken Challenge B out of context, and we apologize to Mr. Berger for this. But we feel that the two short sentences, in *or* out of context, sound a bit choppy. We suggest the use of a comma instead of a period.

[B] Preferred
Most of the credit programs have been created for good reason, but they have gotten out of hand.

Subject/Verb Agreement, Part I: Noise

Challenge A

The cost of all losses not directly charged to Company B are charged back to Company B's divisions through a corporate insurance allocation.

> An analysis of Company B by
> Rotan-Mosle, an investment bank
> in Houston, Texas

Challenge B

Close teamwork provided by our sales, engineering, and research and development departments assure superior service.

> Betz Laboratories, Inc., 1983 annual report

Challenge C

The Board of Directors, with the concurrence of the shareholders, have engaged Ernst & Whinney, independent auditors, to examine the consolidated financial statements of the Company.

> Nalco Corporation 1983 annual report

Challenge D

It is our sensitivity to your investment needs and our agility in helping you reach them that makes us what we are.

> Merrill Lynch "Bull in the China
> Shop" television advertisement

Make the appropriate corrections and read Review 12 to see how you did.

Subject/Verb Agreement, Part I: Noise

The cost is . . .

The costs are . . .

We all know that "is" goes with "cost" while "are" goes with "costs"; the first is singular in construction, and the second is plural. What many of us have problems with is choosing the correct verb when a lot of "noise"—typically prepositional phrases or dependent clauses—separates the subject and the verb of the sentence. Challenge A is a fitting example. "Cost" is the subject, but it is followed by a prepositional phrase and an adjective clause, *i.e.,* noise. Unless the subject is an "apportioning" subject (see Review 14), such noise should *not* affect the selection of the verb. On this basis, the corrected sentences are as follows:

[A] Correct

subject   "noise"   verb

The ⌐cost⌐ of all losses not directly charged to Company B ⌐is⌐ charged back to Company B's divisions through a corporate insurance allocation. [The cost is . . .]

[B] Correct

subject   "noise"

Close ⌐teamwork⌐ provided by our sales, engineering, and re-

verb

search and development departments ⌐assures⌐ superior service. [Close teamwork assures . . .]

[C] Correct

subject   "noise"

The ⌐Board⌐ of Directors, with the concurrence of the sharehold-

verb

ers, ⌐has⌐ engaged Ernst & Whinney . . . [The Board has engaged . . .]

[D] Correct

It is our <u>sensitivity</u> to your investment needs and our <u>*agility*</u> in helping you reach them that <u>*make*</u> us what we are. [Our sensitivity and agility make us what we are.]

(Annotations above the line: "subject #1" over "sensitivity"; "noise" over "to your investment needs"; "subject #2" over "agility"; "noise" over "helping you reach them"; "verb" over "make".)

Subject/Verb Agreement, Part II: More Noise

Challenge A
The production of "Daramic" battery separators in France, as well as the manufacture of fluid cracking catalysts in West Germany, are accomplished with the help of computerized systems to reduce costs and promote consistently high quality.

W. R. Grace & Co. 1982 annual report

Challenge B
This factor, combined with higher prices, new products and services, and unusually strong foreign business, are expected to produce a 15% earning gain.

The Johnson Survey, September 1984

Challenge C
Increased productivity from more highly trained people, together with advanced techniques and state-of-the-art technology such as those employed at the recently completed plant in Lowell, Massachusetts, ensure that we will have capacity available.

Wang Laboratories, Inc., 1982 annual report

Challenge D
A Chicago local, as well as locals in Seattle and Cleveland, back him despite a national union endorsement for Mondale.

"Labor Letter"
The Wall Street Journal, November 6, 1984

Make the appropriate corrections and read Review 13 to see how you did.

Subject/Verb Agreement, Part II: More Noise

When two singular subjects are joined by the word "and" (which is a conjunction), a plural subject is born and a plural verb is required. Note the plural verb "were" in the following sentence:

Their cooperation and support *were* vital.

Such is not the case, however, when we connect nouns by using "as well as," "together with," "along with," "combined with," or "in addition to." These all introduce supplemental information outside the main sentence flow and are really parenthetical in nature (in fact, this type of phrase should always be preceded and followed by a comma). The phrases that these words introduce should be considered "noise." We have coined the term "type-II noise" to describe this type of supplemental information.

So, in Challenge A, the phrase "as well as the manufacture of fluid cracking catalysts in West Germany" is type-II noise and should *not* affect the selection of the verb. The answer to Challenge A, as well as the answers to Challenges B, C, and D, is shown below.

[A] *Correct*

subject   "noise"

The ⌐production⌐ of "Daramic" battery separators in France, as well as the manufacture of fluid cracking catalysts in West
               verb
Germany, ⌐*is*⌐ accomplished with the help of computerized systems... [The production is...]

[B] Correct

This [factor,] [combined with higher prices, new products and services, and unusually strong foreign business,] [*is*] expected to produce a 15% earning gain. [This factor is...]

subject · "noise" · verb

[C] Correct

Increased [productivity] [from more highly trained people, together with advanced techniques and state-of-the-art technology such as those employed at the recently completed plant in Lowell, Massachusetts,] [*ensures*] that we will have capacity available. [Increased productivity ensures...]

subject · "noise" · verb

[D] Correct

A Chicago [local,] [as well as locals in Seattle and Cleveland,] [*backs*] him despite a national union endorsement for Mondale. [A local backs...]

subject · "noise" · verb

Subject/Verb Agreement, Part III: Apportioning Nouns

Challenge A
A very high percentage of our clients produces either foods, drugs, petroleum products, or television entertainment.

A. C. Nielsen 1983 annual report

Challenge B
The remaining 68% of fiscal 1983 revenues was derived from numerous customers.

A report by Rotan-Mosle, an investment bank in Houston, Texas

Challenge C
The number of charges and reversals on past-due invoices has increased over 700%.

Vice-president & director of data processing, DuBois Chemicals

Challenge D
None of Grieve's tactics is new or unique.

Business Week, September 3, 1984

Make the appropriate corrections and read Review 14 to see how you did.

Subject/Verb Agreement, Part III: Apportioning Nouns

"A portion *is*" or "A portion *are*": Which is correct?

There are some nouns in our language—we call them apportioning nouns—that as subjects can take either a singular-form verb or a plural-form verb depending on the noise (see Review 12) that follows them. A non-exhaustive list of commonly used apportioning nouns follows:

> portion
> majority
> some
> 1 percent, 2 percent . . . 100 percent . . .
> most
> plenty
> not any
> a number ⎫
> a percentage ⎬ (explained in detail below)
> a proportion ⎭
> none (explained in detail below)

The noise that immediately follows these apportioning nouns generally consists of the word "of" and an object. The apportioning noun indicates what portion of this object we are talking about.

> 18 percent of the firms ⟹ tells what portion of the firms we are talking about
> Most of the directors ⟹ tells what portion of the directors we are talking about

So, when are these apportioning nouns considered plural and when are they considered singular? Well, the apportioning noun is considered plural if the object following "of" is plural:

[A] Correct
A very high percentage of our client*s produce* ...

[B] Correct
The remaining 68% of fiscal 1983 revenue*s were* ...

And it is considered singular if the object following "of" is singular:

A high percentage of the *fluid produces* valuable by-products.
The remaining 68% of the *increase was* ...

The thing to watch out for when applying this rule is an apportioning noun that is preceded by "the" and that refers to *one* specific number:

The number of directors in this committee *has* increased.
The percentage of acute-care hospitals operated by for-profit chains *is* increasing.
The proportion of salt in the mixture *has* declined.

Note that a singular verb is used whether the object following "of" is plural ("directors," "hospitals") or singular ("salt"). So, while "a percentage," "a proportion," and "a number" are apportioning nouns, the "the" versions of each are not. Challence C is a perfect example: "The number" in this excerpt is not an apportioning noun. Rather, the phrase refers to one specific number and must therefore take a singular verb. Thus, the statement is correct as written:

[C] Correct [No correction needed.]
The number of charges and reversals on past-due invoices has increased over 700%.

If, however, we were to substitute "A" for "The" in the above example, we would need a plural verb. (We would also have to change the meaning of the sentence, as shown below.)

A number of charges and reversals on past-due invoices *have been made.*

Concerning the apportioning noun "none," you undoubtedly have been taught somewhere that the word always takes a singular verb (because, the rationale goes, "none" means "no one" or "not one"). We—and most experts—believe, however, that "none" generally is used to mean "not any"; and "not any" is an apportioning noun, taking a singular verb only when the object following the "of" is singular:

None of the work *was* done by me.
None of that forest *was* damaged.

If the object is plural, though, then "none" takes a plural verb (this is most often the case):

None of the products *were* as good as ours.

Concerning Challenge D specifically:

[D] Correct
None of Grieve's tactics *are* new or unique.

Note: If you want to emphasize the singular—that is, you really mean "not one" rather than "not any"—then you're better off saying "not one" rather than "none":

Not one [rather than "none"] of Grieve's tactics *is* new or unique.

Subject/Verb Agreement,
Part IV: Singular Dollars

Challenge A
Over $400,000 were spent in TV advertising last year on that
product.

> Account executive of an adver-
> tising company

Challenge B
At least $200,000 of the savings were wasted on that one
project.

> Product manager of a huge con-
> sumer products concern

*Make the appropriate corrections and read Review 15 to see how
you did.*

Subject/Verb Agreement, Part IV: Singular Dollars

Dollar figures, despite their plural facade, are generally considered to be singular, because the figure is viewed as a *single sum* of money rather than as so many individual dollars.

[A] Correct
Over $400,000 *was* spent...

[B] Correct
At least $200,000... *was* wasted...

An exception, of course, is in those rare cases where you *are* referring to the individual dollar bills (or the individual cents/pennies, etc.).

Subject/Verb Agreement,
Part V: Last but Not Least

Challenge A
Neither the execution by Seller or Stockholder of this Agreement nor the documents to be executed by Seller and Stockholder in connection herewith violates the Articles of Incorporation.

> Acquisition agreement between Fortune 500 company and small, private company

Challenge B
Neither Washington nor Iran are able to confirm that.

> Anchorwoman, NBC affiliate

Challenge C
No representation, promise, inducement, or statement of intentions have been made.

> Letter from lawyer representing medium-size company in San Diego

Make the appropriate corrections and read Review 16 to see how you did.

Subject/Verb Agreement,
Part V: Last but Not Least

Whether the verb following the phrase "neither...nor..." takes the singular form or the plural form depends on whether the nearest noun (in most cases, this means the last noun) of the compound subject is singular or plural:

[A] Correct

last noun is plural...   ...so the verb is plural

Neither the execution...nor the ‾documents‾...‾*violate*‾ the Articles of Incorporation.

As shown above, when the nearest noun is plural, so, too, is the verb. Had the nearest noun been singular ("document"), though, the correct verb would have been singular, too ("violates").

Challenge B is no different:

[B] Correct

singular   singular

Neither Washington nor ‾Iran‾ ‾*is*‾ able to confirm that.

This "last-noun" principle also applies to the following types of compound subjects:

1. or	A, b, or c is/are typically chosen.
2. no...or...	No d, e, or f is/are warranted
3. either...or...	Either g or h is/are sufficient.

As with "neither...nor...," the verb selection in the three cases above should be governed by the last noun (c, f, and h, respectively).

[C] Correct

last noun is singular...

No representation, promise, inducement, or ⌐statement¬ of inten-

...so the verb is singular

tions ⌐has¬ been made.

"Lastly" Is Least

Challenge A

More importantly, Bendix opens the door for expansion of some Allied business.

> Allied Corporation 1983 annual report

Challenge B

Thirdly, I want to talk a little bit about our growth strategy.

> The chairman of Economic Laboratories, Inc.
> Brochure covering the annual meeting of stockholders, November 9, 1984

Challenge C

Just as importantly is the report of an honest attempt to build a serious American automobile to world-class standards.

> Editor-at-large
> BMW *Roundel Magazine*, October 1984

Make the appropriate corrections and read Review 17 to see how you did.

"Lastly" Is Least

We believe you should avoid introducing a sentence with "more importantly" (or with any phrase containing the word "importantly"). "What's more" or "more important" both sound much cleaner and more concise. Besides which, the complete clause is "What is more important." And no one would say, "What is more importantly."

Also, avoid saying "secondly," "thirdly," etc., to introduce sentences or paragraphs in a sequence. First, they are terribly clumsy words. Second, if you ever make it up to "twelfthly" and "thirteenthly," you'll cringe at the thought of using such monstrosities. Third, unless you start out with "firstly" instead of "first" (and who ever says "firstly"?), you are being inconsistent.

Let's now correct the Challenge statements.

[A] Correct
More *important*, Bendix opens the door for expansion of some Allied business.

[B] Correct
Third, I want to talk a little bit about our growth strategy.

[C] Correct
Just as *important* is the report of an honest attempt to build a serious American automobile to world-class standards.

By the way, also avoid "lastly"; use "last" instead.

Numbers: Spell Out or Use Figures?

Challenge A
Before the 15-member board came up with its three-percent figure, the advisors were suggesting four and one-half percent, and certain independent estimates were fluctuating between 2.2% and five percent.

> Report of a graduate business student

Challenge B
Approximately ten million shares were traded that day.

> A stockbroker's letter

Challenge C
25.2% of the stockholders tendered their shares.

> Stock analyst

Make the appropriate corrections and read Review 18 to see how you did.

Numbers: Spell Out or Use Figures?

The "experts" disagree on when to write out a number (forty-five) and when to use the figure (45) instead. Many textbooks suggest using figures for any number over ten, but we regard the issue as more complex than that. The decision to use the figure or to spell out the number is dependent on two things: the type of number and the context—quantitative or non-quantitative—in which the number appears. *Note:* Examples of quantitative contexts: "6% inflation"; "sales increase of 11%"; "price-earnings multiple of 9." Examples of non-quantitative contexts: "nine sales reps retired"; "three alternatives"; "eighteen members of the board." A decision matrix for the "spell out vs. use figures" controversy is shown on the following page.

Note in the facing exhibit that some flexibility is provided in certain circumstances. For instance, when a cluster (defined as three or more numbers appearing in the same phrase or sentence) of one- or two-digit numbers appears in a *non-quantitative* context, either you can spell out the numbers or, for reasons of conciseness, you can use figures. Whichever you choose in these circumstances, be consistent—a mixture of figures and written-out numbers in a comparable context is distracting. This same consistency rule applies to "round" numbers of three or more digits (such as "6,000" or "six thousand") in a non-quantitative context: Make a decision and apply it across the board. In addition, be consistent in your use of decimals when referring to quantities of similar items, *i.e.,* do not say, "There was a 14.5% [note: only one digit to the right of the decimal] increase in territory Y and a 5.375% [note: three digits after the decimal] increase in territory Z." Finally, be consistent in your use of "%" versus "percent" and in your use of "% pt." versus "percentage point."

Context	Type of Number		
	1 or 2 Digits	*3 or More Digits*	*Decimals*
Context *Quantitative* (financial, statistical, or scientific data)	Use figures.	Use figures (for round numbers in the millions or billions, use a combination: "45 million").	Use figures.
Non-Quantitative	Spell out (unless the numbers appear in clusters; then you may want to use figures).	Use figures (unless the numbers are round numbers [hundreds, thousands, etc.]; then you may want to spell out).	Use figures.

Before we begin analyzing the Challenges, let us warn you that there is sometimes a fuzzy distinction between a quantitative context and a non-quantitative context. The only advice we can give for such situations is this: Use your best judgment and be consistent.

Now for the Challenges.

[A] Correct
Before the *fifteen*-member [non-quantitative context] board came up with its *3.0%* figure, the advisors were suggesting *4.5%*, and certain independent estimates were fluctuating between *2.2%* and *5.0%* [a cluster of numbers in a quantitative context].

Note that although one of the numbers in the above example is spelled out and some are expressed as figures, this is *not* inconsistent. Simply, the first number appears in a non-quantitative context and the others in a quantitative (statistical) context. (Yes, two different contexts in one sentence.)

The "ten million" in Challenge B represents one of those gray areas—the context could be considered quantitative or non-quantitative. For this reason, Challenge B is correct as it stands, but substituting "10 million" for "ten million" would in no way be incorrect. Avoid, however, the use of "10,000,000"; leave these long-winded figures to the accountants.

[B] Correct [No correction needed.]
Approximately ten million shares were traded that day.

Also Correct
Approximately *10* million shares were traded that day.

Challenge C brings us to the major exception to the rules discussed above: You shouldn't *begin* a sentence with a figure. Instead, we suggest writing out the number, unless the number is a decimal or unless the number is so long that it looks awkward in written-out form or unless writing out the number would result in an unbearable sacrifice of consistency. In such cases, recast the sentence so that a non-number begins the sentence.

With the above in mind, we recommend rewriting Challenge C ("25.2%" can hardly be written out). A few suggestions:

[C] Recommended
Just over 25% of the shareholders tendered their shares.

Also Recommended
Approximately one-fourth (25.2%) of the shareholders tendered their shares.

Also Recommended
Officially, 25.2% of the shareholders tendered their shares.

Perilous Non-Parallels

Challenge A
Nalco Cetane Improvers help diesel engines start easier in cold
weather, run smoother, and have reduced emissions.

> Nalco Corporation 1983 annual
> report

Challenge B
The central thrust of our strategy is to capitalize on deregulation
with the primary objective of forging an organization geared not
only to be a surviving institution but a profitable one well into
the future.

> First Interstate Bancorp 1982 an-
> nual report

Challenge C
...680 recommendations totalling $103.5 billion in three-year
PPSS savings have either been included in the budget baseline
for fiscal years 1983, 1984, or 1985 or are currently targeted for
short-term implementation.

> J. Peter Grace, chairman of W.
> R. Grace & Co. and chairman
> of Chemed Corporation, in a
> letter to Albert L. Kraus, editor
> of *The Journal of Commerce*

Challenge D

AEIBC is known for helping companies cut through the foreign trade tangle, either in exporting their goods or undertaking major construction projects.

American Express 1983 annual report

Make the appropriate corrections and read Review 19 to see how you did.

Perilous Non-Parallels

Words, phrases, or clauses are considered parallel when their overall grammatical structure is balanced. As Theodore Bernstein put it in *The Careful Writer:* "This is merely the equivalent of saying that you should not harness a horse and a dachshund to the same plow, nor design the facade for a building with three Doric columns on one side of the entrance and one Corinthian column on the other." Although it *sounds* simple enough, it appears from our experience (of finding literally hundreds of examples of this type of error) that while the average business person can balance his accounts, balance his career and family, and balance his checkbook(s), he simply cannot balance his sentence structures. Such a pitfall results in illogical and unclear sentences that reflect unfavorably on the writer.

The need for parallelism arises whenever words, phrases, or clauses are joined by conjunctions:

Single Conjunctions	Specific Examples	General Construction (*Note*: Only *one* conjunction exists in each example)
but	Jack was there, but Debby wasn't.	*a1,* but *a2*
and	Gregg, Keith, and John will attend.	*a1, a2,* and *a3*
	Calvin was smiling, and so was Mary.	*a1,* and *a2*
or	I'll give it to Jill or Shawn.	*a1* or *a2*

Double Conjunctions	Specific Examples	General Construction (*Note:* Two conjunctions per example)
both . . . and	Both Lisa and Tara will be there.	both *a1* and *a2*
either . . . or	Either Randy or Tip will go.	either *a1* or *a2*
not only . . . but	We won not only the battle, but also the war.	not only *a1*, but (also) *a2*

In the above examples, all the *a1*'s must be structurally equivalent to the *a2*'s. This means that if *a1* starts with a preposition ("in," "on," "through," "with," "to," "from," etc.) then so must *a2*; if *a1* starts with a verb then so must *a2*; and . . . well, you get the picture. (If you don't get the picture, don't worry: The simple testing procedures outlined below allow you, in most cases, to judge quickly and easily if a sentence structure is balanced.)

Regarding single conjunctions (*e.g.*, *a1* and *a2*), the testing procedure is straightforward. First, line up the *a1*'s with the *a2*'s (and, in many cases, with the *a3*'s, too) and then test "by sight." Testing by sight simply entails comparing the various phrases for structural equivalence (*i.e.*, parallelism). Let's use Challenge A as an example.

Nalco Cetane Improvers help
diesel engines
- start easier
- run smoother (and)
- have reduced emissions

The third phrase is not in sync with the first two phrases because the first two are written in active voice while the third is written in passive voice. This creates an awkward and difficult-to-read sentence. There are several possible ways to provide balance (and smoothness) to this sentence; one recommendation follows:

[A] Recommended
Nalco Cetane Improvers help diesel engines start easier, run smoother, and *emit fewer pollutants* [or perhaps, for public relations reasons, we might want to use "give off fewer emissions"].

Regarding double conjunctions (*e.g.*, not only *a1* but *a2*), checking for parallelism is conceptually no different from doing so with single conjunctions, but this time we use a testing technique we call "restructure-then-test." To restructure, find the two conjunctions in the sentence and *exclude* them and anything in between them from the sentence. Then, simply test the sentence to see if it makes sense in its restructured form. This technique works, and this is important to remember, because everything *before* the first conjunction is *shared* by both *a1* and *a2*.

Let's try this restructure-then-test technique on Challenge B. Here is Challenge B as it exists on page 65:

> The central thrust of our strategy is to capitalize on deregulation with the primary objective of forging an organization geared not only to be a surviving institution but a profitable one well into the future.

To restructure, we must first find the two conjunctions: They are "not only" and "but." Now we must exclude these conjunctions and everything in between them from the sentence:

> The central thrust of our strategy is to capitalize on deregulation, with the primary objective of forging an organization geared ⌈ excluded part . . . ⌉ a profitable one well into the future.

Now, let's reread the restructured version to test it. The sentence doesn't seem to make much sense, does it? The reason is a lack of parallelism. Notice that the verb phrase "to be" follows the first conjunction but not the second. To remedy this case of the "Perilous Non-Parallels," we need either to place "to be" *before* the first conjunction, whereby the phrase will be shared by both *a1* and *a2,* or to add a second "to be" after the second conjunction. Both of these remedies are shown below.

[B] Correct
... with the primary objective of forging an organization geared *to be not only* a surviving institution but a profitable one well into the future.

Also Correct
... with the primary objective of forging an organization geared *not only to be* a surviving institution but *to be* a profitable one well into the future.

Let's now try Challenge C. Here's the sentence in its un-restructured form:

> ... 680 recommendations totalling $103.5 billion in three-year PPSS savings have either been included in the budget baseline for fiscal years 1983, 1984, and 1985 or are currently targeted for short-term implementation.

And now here it is in its restructured form:

> ... 680 recommendations totalling $103.5 billion in three-year PPSS savings have ⌐ . . . ¬ are currently targeted for short-term implementation.

(*excluded part*)

The restructured version above makes no sense: "PPSS savings *have are* targeted..."? The lack of parallelism is once again evident, the problem being that "have" is shared by both *a1* ("been included in the budget") and *a2* ("are currently targeted for short-term implementation"). Unfortunately, *a2* does not contain a "been" to round out the "have been" phrase. Our recommendation, then, is either to place the "have" inside *a1* (where it's not shared) or to add a "been" to *a2* so that it reads "been targeted for short-term implementation." These suggestions are shown below.

[C] Correct
... 680 recommendations totalling $103.5 billion in three-year PPSS savings *either have been* included in the budget or are currently targeted for short-term implementation.

Also Correct
... 680 recommendations totalling $103.5 billion in three-year PPSS savings *have either been* included in the budget or *been* targeted for short-term implementation.

Try Challenge D on your own. You will notice that it is incorrect for reasons similar to the ones discussed above. Listed below are two recommended solutions.

[D] Correct:
AEIBC is known for helping companies cut through the foreign trade tangle, either in exporting their goods or *in* undertaking major construction projects.

Also Correct
AEIBC is known for helping companies cut through the foreign trade tangle, *in either* exporting their goods or undertaking major construction projects.

Give "Me" Some Respect

Challenge A
My goal in my first year was to add substance to the telecast by telling why players and teams were effective. The next thing is for Dick [Stockton] and I to become more comfortable as a team.

> Tommy Heinsohn in an interview as summarized by Rudy Bartzke
> *USA Today*, September 21, 1984

Challenge B
Between you and I . . .

> Heard all the time—from the local pub to Fortune 500 board rooms. In fact, we heard such a statement on the TV program *Cheers*, murmured by none other than "Grammar Queen" Diane.

Challenge C
Roger Mudd will join John Chancellor and I after this message . . .

> Tom Brokaw in his commentary following the first presidential debate, October 7, 1984

Make the appropriate corrections and read Review 20 to see how you did.

Give "Me" Some Respect

This lesson is actually a subset of the "Perilous Non-Parallels" lesson, but we thought it deserved special mention...thus, a lesson of its own.

In their attempts to eliminate the phrase "Susan and me" (as in "Susan and me want to go swimming"), parents and elementary schoolteachers alike have brainwashed an entire generation into firmly believing that "Susan and *I*" is the sophisticate's phrasing while "Susan and *me*" is simply illiterate. The truth is, however, that the phrase "Susan and me" (or "John and me" or "'Whomever' and me") has been much maligned. As a *noun phrase,* "Susan and me" is indeed wrong ("Susan and I went swimming" is correct). But in several other circumstances— such as prepositional phrases and dual direct objects, for example— "Susan and me" is correct and the use of "Susan and I" would be incorrect. Read on for further insight.

When there is only one object of a preposition, most business people have no trouble:

Correct	**Not Correct**
...thought of *me*	...thought of *I*
...given to *him*	...given to *he*
...passed by *her*	...passed by *she*
...dumped on *them*	...dumped on *they*
...communicated through *us*	...communicated through *we*

Many business people have much more difficulty, however, when there are two or more objects of a preposition. But dealing with two or more objects should really be no more difficult than dealing with one. Just as you would never say "John's performance was evaluated by *I*," you would never say "John's performance was evaluated by *Susan and I*" (the "I" should be "me" in both cases). Once again, testing is the easiest and most effective way to determine which word is the correct one to use. As before, it is necessary to restructure before testing:

John's performance was evaluated by--<

Susan (and)

I

(*Note:* When restructuring, remember to "parenthesize" conjunctions and to disregard them when reading each phrase.)

To test, we simply separate the sentence into two phrases:

John's performance was evaluated by Susan.
John's performance was evaluated by I.

At this point, the error becomes evident.

Let's now do the same with Challenge A. First, we restructure:

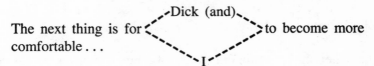

The next thing is for
comfortable . . .
Dick (and)
I
to become more

Then we test:

The next thing is for Dick to become more comfortable.
The next thing is for I to become more comfortable.

By testing, we discover that Mr. Heinsohn, too, has been brainwashed. The correct choice is, of course, "me":

[A] Correct
The next thing is for Dick and *me* to become more comfortable...

The above restructuring technique will work with (and should be used in the case of) all prepositions save a few. The one exception deserving special mention is the preposition "between." Because restructuring makes little sense in this particular case, you simply will have to de-program yourself by remembering that every time you say "between you and I," you are really saying "between we," and that sounds terribly odd...moreover, it's incorrect. (*Note:* "You and I" is equivalent to "we," while "you and me" is equivalent to "us.")

[B] Correct
Between you and *me*...

"ME" AS AN OBJECT OF A VERB

These same principles apply when dealing with objects of a verb. Just as you would never say "John thought of I" ("me," not "I," should be the object of the preposition "of"), you would never say "John took I" ("me" should be the object of the verb "took"). The rules do not change when dealing with *two* objects of a verb. Our standard test proves the point:

John took Diane and *me* to court.

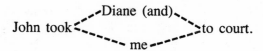

John took Diane (and) me to court.

Challenge C is an interesting example, as it was witnessed by millions of folks on TV:

[C] Correct

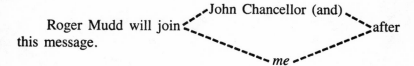

Roger Mudd will join John Chancellor (and) *me* after this message.

"Myself" Misfits

Challenge A

Tracy and myself agreed that without some organic context, the business letter can become artificial and intrusive.

An MBA friend of ours

Challenge B

Please join Norma Rashid and myself at 6:00 and at 11:00.

Anchorman, NBC affiliate

Challenge C

The volume-analysis study undertaken by IBM and ourselves concluded that our transaction rate is 1,760 per hour during peak loads.

Data processing manager of a
Fortune 500 company

Make the appropriate corrections and read Review 21 to see how you did.

"Myself" Misfits

Words ending in "-self" or "-selves" are called reflexives. There are only two situations when reflexives should be used:

1. When emphasis is wanted:

I, myself, did it.
The secretaries put it together themselves.

2. When one does something to one's self:

I kicked myself for speaking incorrectly in front of the boss.
I feel certain that my boss was thinking to himself that I should literally be kicked.

Note in the above examples that whenever "myself" is used, "I" is mentioned earlier in the sentence; and when "himself" is used, "he" (or whomever "himself" refers to) is mentioned earlier in the sentence; and the same applies to "herself," "themselves," and "ourselves." In fact, this little rule serves as the basis for our test: Never use a *reflexive* word if it is not *reflected*, earlier in the sentence, by the word it refers to. (*Note:* Sometimes the word is *reflected* but does not actually appear. An example is "Do it yourself." In an imperative construction such as this, the reflected word "you" does not appear but is implied, as in "[You] do it yourself.")

Now for the Challenge statements.

Never use "myself" as the subject of a sentence. To illustrate, let's apply the test described on page 74 to Challenge A.

Tracy
(and)   agreed that without some organic context, the
myself   business letter can become artificial and intrusive.

Obviously, "myself agreed..." is incorrect; the word "I"
should replace the word "myself."

[A] Correct
Tracy and *I* agreed...

Challenge B is incorrect because "myself" does not reflect
anything in the sentence. This can be seen clearly in the
following test.

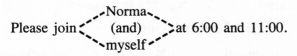

Please join   Norma
                (and)   at 6:00 and 11:00.
                myself

Application of the test shows that "myself" is incorrect
("please join myself"?) and that "me" (as in "please join
me") is correct.

[B] Correct
Please join Norma Rashid and me at 6:00 and 11:00.

Challenge C is incorrect because, once again, the reflexive
word does not reflect anything. The word "ourselves" would be
correct only if "we" had appeared earlier in the sentence (*i.e.*,
"*We* undertook the study *ourselves*"). Since "we" does not
appear, the correct word is "us," as in "The... study undertak-
en by IBM and by us concluded that..."

[C] Correct
The volume-analysis study undertaken by IBM and *us* concluded that our transaction rate is 1,760 per hour during peak loads.

Because the correct version above sounds a bit awkward, you
may want to consider restructuring the sentence.

Correct and Smooth
The volume-analysis study *that we undertook* with IBM
concluded...

GOOD GRAMMAR at a GLANCE
CHALLENGE 22

"The Data Is" ... Incorrect!

Challenge A
Data is based on a sample of properties from the *National Trend of Business in the Economy Lodging Industry.*

> *National Trend of Business: Lodging Industry,* a publication of Laventhal & Horwath

Challenge B
Although 75% of the senior executives use the data to plan for the company, experts say all data is underused.

> Cathy Trost, "Labor Letter"
> *The Wall Street Journal,*
> August 28, 1983

Challenge C
Because Company X was formed in October of 1982, only one year of historical data has been included.

> One of the authors of this book (we won't say which one) in a Chemed board memorandum, November 1983

Challenge D
The media should attempt to censor itself.

> WEBN (radio station) roundtable discussion, November 4, 1984

Make the appropriate corrections and read Review 22 to see how you did.

"The Data Is"... Incorrect!

As implied by the title of this review, the phrase "the data is" is incorrect, for "data" is the plural form of "datum" (a single piece of data). Thus, you would say the following:

[A] Correct
Data *are* based on a sample...

[B] Correct
...all data *are* underused.

If you are not comfortable with the word "datum," try "a piece of data (is)" or "one item in the data (is)" or even "the information (is)" when the singular is required.

The principle above also applies to the following commonly misused terms:

singular form	**plural form**
criterion	criteria
medium	media
phenomenon	phenomena

Contrary to the examples above, the word "agenda" has departed from its original meaning of things to be done and now means a *program* of things to be done; as a result "agenda" has become singular in nature and "agendas" is the correct plural form.

As for Challenges C and D, the answers are shown below.

[C] Correct [No correction needed.]
...only one year of historical data has been included.

This one was included to keep you alert. "Year"—not "data"—is the subject of the sentence; thus, "has"—not "have" —is the correct verb. (See Review 12 on "noise.")

[D] Correct
The media (plural form) should attempt to censor *themselves* (needs to be plural also).

A Company: It or They?

Challenge A

Company X is willing to pay six times book value because they want to stake out a position in the mail order business and, more important, they want to shore-up their sagging fourth quarter earnings.

> President and CEO in a memorandum to the chairman of a Fortune 100 company

Challenge B

Company X is willing to pay six times book value because it wants to stake out a position in the mail order business, and, more important, it wants to shore-up its sagging fourth quarter earnings.

> Challenge A, revised

Challenge C

Claire Manufacturing supplies the nationwide sanitary supply market under their own name.

> Oakite Products, Inc., 1983 annual report

Challenge D

Claire Manufacturing supplies the nationwide sanitary supply market under its own name.

> Challenge C, revised

Make the appropriate corrections and read Review 23 to see how you did.

A Company: It or They?

Note in Challenge A that the subject company, Company X, takes a *singular* verb ("is") but later in the sentence is referred to as "they" (a *plural* entity), rather than "it." Obviously, such a practice is inconsistent. Take a look, though, at Challenge B. Here, the "consistent" alternative sounds stilted; "it" doesn't appear natural in place of "they." The same holds true for Challenge D, the consistent alternative to the inconsistent Challenge C.

The consistent approach—referring to a company as an "it" —is never wrong. "It" may sound a bit inappropriate in some informal settings, but it's not wrong. We feel, however, the inconsistent approach is also acceptable, at least in more informal situations. Thus, all of the Challenge statements are "correct" when written in informal contexts, but, in "formal" writing (such as annual reports), only Challenges B and D would be acceptable.

[A], [C] Comment
Acceptable in informal contexts only.

[B], [D] Comment
Acceptable as written.

The rule above applies not only to companies, but to a host of other "collective nouns":

department (the department reached its/their goal)	subsidiary
	unit
division	management
board (of directors)	clientele
committee	

Be Real

Challenge A
They are among the nation's 2.37 million farmers who are struggling to pay interest on total liabilities that have soared 63 percent since 1979, from $132 billion to $215 billion.

> William Robbins, "Despair Wrenches Farmers' Lives as Debts Mount and Land Is Lost" *The New York Times*, February 10, 1985

Make the appropriate corrections and read Review 24 to see how you did.

Be Real

Because inflation is now ingrained in our lives, we must account for it accordingly. Accounting for it means putting increases—of dollar amounts—into perspective. So, when total liabilities increase from $132 billion in 1979 to $215 billion, as stated in Challenge A, we must look at two rates of increase: the nominal rate (for which no adjustments are made) of 63% and the *real rate* (adjusted for inflation) of 14%.

Note: To determine this real rate of growth we use this formula:

$$\frac{1 + \text{nominal growth rate}}{1 + \text{inflation rate}} - 1$$

Notice that the real rate of growth over the last five years was only 14%, which translates into an average real growth rate per year of less than 3%. Now, this *does* represent a real increase, and we are certain that the nation's farmers are indeed struggling to pay this increased burden of liabilities. But to say that the total liability level "soared" is stretching it. We're not suggesting actually *including* both the nominal rate and the real rate of increase (or decrease) in your writing. We're simply suggesting being conscious of inflation and its effect on *real* rates of growth by putting your dollar increases into perspective.

[A] Preferred
They are among the nation's 2.37 million farmers who are struggling to pay interest on total liabilities that have *increased* 63 percent since 1979, from $132 billion to $215 billion.

or

They are among the nation's 2.37 million farmers who are struggling to pay interest on total liabilities that have increased 63 percent as compared with total farm revenues, which have increased at a marginal 27 percent rate over the same time period.

To make your "putting growth into perspective" task easier, we have included the primary macro-economic indices in Appendix A.

Placement, However, Is Difficult

Challenge A
Division P's retention rate [the rate of salesperson retention] declined to 89.9% in 1983 from 92.3% in 1982. However, this lower rate must be viewed in light of the Division's 1982 manpower strategy.

Stock analyst

Challenge B
That decision [to transfer all programs from the NCR Century 201 to the Criterion] significantly increased the cost of operation for the Criterion, however, we were able to save about $3,000 per month in NCR Century 201 maintenance fees.

Data processing manager of a
$100-million-plus corporation

Challenge C
Wang, like any large commercial enterprise, has complex financial strategies which are difficult to reduce to simple definitions. However, there are some specific areas which showed significant results.

Wang 1983 annual report

Make the appropriate corrections and read Review 25 to see how you did.

Placement, However, Is Difficult

There are two things one should know about the word "however."

1. "However" is used to express a contrast between two elements or ideas occurring in two consecutive clauses or sentences:

She is good; he, however, is bad.

Thus, the word "however" should be placed where it most clearly emphasizes the desired contrast. Such a placement will always be in the *second* clause or sentence, but finding just the right place within this second clause or sentence is sometimes difficult. Most often, but not always, the most effective placement is in the *middle* of the sentence, immediately following the contrasted element. Such a placement in the middle of the sentence will typically (but, once again, not always) provide a more effective contrast and a better sentence flow than the placement of "however" at the beginning of the sentence— compare the sentence below with the similar one above and notice how the oomph of the contrast is lost:

Avoid: She is good; however, he is bad.

2. When "however" begins the second clause of a compound sentence, it must be preceded by a semicolon (see second example in rule 1 above).

With these two rules in mind, let's now determine what is wrong with the Challenges on the previous page.

Challenge A is not wrong, per se. We do feel, however,

that the contrast could be more effectively highlighted by a "re-placement" of the word "however":

[A] Correct
Division P's retention rate declined to 89.9% in 1983 from 92.3% in 1982. This lower rate must be viewed, *however,* in light of the Division's 1982 manpower strategy.

As for Challenge B, the excerpt is definitely wrong, for the sentence violates rule 2 described above. In this case, the two clauses are closely linked in meaning, so a semicolon must be used. In addition, we would recommend a "re-placement" of "however":

[B] Correct
That decision . . . significantly increased the cost of operation for the Criterion; these increased costs were partially offset, *however,* by the $3,000 reduction in NCR maintenance fees.

Challenge C is loaded with problems (it's just poor "Wanguage"). To begin with, both "which's" should be "that's," but we'll leave that for Review 5. Moreover, this paragraph is a perfect example of the careless use of "however" to attempt to link ideas that are unrelated. The implication in this paragraph is that "showing significant results" is in contrast with the "difficulty to reduce to simple definitions."

[C] Comment
We suggest a rewrite to clarify the contrast, if any, between the two ideas. (Also, both "which's" should be "that's.")

The Big IF

Challenge A
If I was you...

Heard too often

Make the appropriate correction and read Review 26 to see how you did.

The Big IF

When we introduce a clause with "if," "as though," or the verb "to wish," we oftentimes *suppose* things that are not the case.

If I were President . . . [but I am not].
He acted as though he were President [but he is not].
She wishes she were President [but she is not].

When such suppositions are expressed in a past tense, it is necessary to use the verb "were," whether we're dealing with a singular noun (as we were in all three examples above) or a plural noun.

It may sound as if we are being terribly picky with this rule, but there *is* some logic to it. You see, the word "if," used with the past tense, has two functions: to express uncertainty, as in, "If the butler was in the house [but we're not certain if he was or not], then he did it"; and to express a supposition, as discussed above.

The telltale sign that differentiates the two possible meanings (at least in the case where a singular noun is used) is the tense of the verb. "Was" is used to express uncertainty; "were" to express a supposition.

If ever in doubt as to which one to use, refer to the following when-in-doubt rule: *Whenever you can state* with certainty *that the phrase beginning with "if" is not true, then you have supposed something and you need to use "were" rather than "was."*

The answer to Challenge A is shown below.

[A] Correct

If I *were* you . . . [but I am certain that I am not; therefore, "were" is correct].

Apostrophes: Possessing a Working Knowledge

Challenge A
It's biggest weakness is a dependence on the general economy.

> Financial staff member of a major corporation

Challenge B
I believe he is a man who's word can be trusted.

> Letter from an acquisition broker

Challenge C
Illinois's employment picture has brightened significantly.

> Brochure from a corporate relocation company

Challenge D
My computers' inability to "talk" with his made things difficult.

> Staff analyst of a mid-size corporation (he has only one computer)

Make the appropriate corrections and read Review 27 to see how you did.

Apostrophes: Possessing a Working Knowledge

One of the more common—and one of the more glaring—errors found in business writing is misuse of the apostrophe. The specific case that accounts for at least fifty percent of these errors is highlighted in Challenges A and B. The corrected versions of these Challenges are shown below:

[A] Correct
Its biggest weakness is a dependence on the general economy.

[B] Correct
I believe he is a man *whose* word can be trusted.

We were all taught to form the possessive of a word by adding an apostrophe and an "s." Unfortunately, there are certain pronouns that are already possessive and do not require the use of an apostrophe *and* an "s." Most writers have no trouble with "hers," "ours," etc. (*i.e.*, you don't often see "her's" or "our's"), but they do have considerable trouble with "its" and "whose." These apostrophe-happy people have a tendency to write the contractions "it's" (meaning "it is") and "who's" (meaning "who is") when they really want the possessives "its" and "whose." This can be terribly confusing for a reader. So, remember, "it's" is the contracted version of "it is," not the possessive form of "it"; and "who's" is the contracted version of "who is," *not* the possessive form of "who."

A second area of confusion surrounding apostrophes involves possessives of words ending in "s" or in an "s"-sound: Do you add just an apostrophe or do you add both an apostrophe and an "s"? Grammar books recommend adding an apostrophe and an "s" to singular words ("boy" becomes "boy's") and adding just an apostrophe to plural words ("boys" becomes "boys' "). This rule, however, can lead to difficulty for the reader, as illustrated by Challenge C, where a singular word, "Illinois," has been made possessive by adding both an apostrophe and an "s." Unfortunately, with this additional "s," the word is not pronounced/read the same way it is written. As a result of this potential confusion, we recommend the following when-in-doubt rule: *When forming the possessive of a word that ends in an "s" or "s"-sound, add an apostrophe and an additional "s" only if the sound of this additional "s" is actually pronounced when saying the possessive. Otherwise, just add the apostrophe.* Of course, the pronunciation of certain words is open to debate; our only advice is to use your best judgment and to be careful not to produce an awkward-sounding phrase through the use of the "apostrophe 's' " combination. Thus Challenge C should be:

[C] Correct
Illinois' employment picture has brightened significantly.

A final problem associated with the use of apostrophes is the correct placement of the apostrophe. This is usually the result of careless writing. Many writers do not take the time to make sure that what they have written (or what has been typed) is what they want to communicate. Challenge D is an example of this. The corrected version is shown below.

[D] Correct
My computer's inability to "talk" with his made things difficult.

"Computers' " probably made it through because it looks like it is correct, although in this sentence "computer's" is the correct word. Just remember to be careful in placing apostrophes, and proofread.

Commas, Commas, and More Commas

Challenge A

... worked together to develop a coating that helps electrodes last longer thus reducing replacement costs.

> Nalco Corporation 1983 annual report

Challenge B

The IV nursing services program has grown from 2 contracts in 1980, to 5 at the end of 1981 and to 14 contracts at the end of 1982.

> Omnicare, Inc., 1982 annual report

Challenge C

Moreover, Omnicare operates within a broad cross-section of the health care industry and all of its businesses are relatively recession-resistant.

> Omnicare, Inc., 1982 annual report

Challenge D

After the acquisition, the company will be involved in three businesses: first aid supplies, janitor supplies and cleaning equipment and safety equipment.

> Investment bank report

Make the appropriate corrections and read Review 28 to see how you did.

Commas, Commas, and More Commas

Almost every writer has problems with commas at one time or another. They are used primarily to separate words or clauses from each other so as to make sentences easier for the reader to understand. Usually the sound of a sentence as it is intended by the writer to be read is a good guide to placement of commas within a sentence: A comma is normally needed wherever a speaker would pause if the sentence were spoken. This can be seen clearly in Challenge A, the corrected version of which is shown below:

[A] Correct
... worked together to develop a coating that helps electrodes last longer, thus reducing replacement costs.

The comma added to this Challenge causes the reader to pause after "longer," allowing him to see that an additional idea (reduced replacement costs) is about to be introduced. Without the comma the reader has a tendency to forge ahead into the reduced-replacement-cost idea and get confused as to the writer's meaning. The reader then has to reread the end of the sentence to be sure of its meaning.

Oftentimes it is the overuse—rather than non-use—of commas that makes a writer's work difficult to read. Commas should be used only where they are needed to help the reader. An example of the overused comma is seen in Challenge B.

[B] Correct
The IV nursing services program has grown from 2 contracts in 1980 to 5 at the end of 1981 and to 14 contracts at the end of 1982.

The comma in the original version is a hindrance to the

reader and was stuck in apparently because the writer thought this was a series of items that needed a comma. If we eliminate the "noise," however, the sentence reads: ". . . grown from 2 contracts . . . to 5 [contracts] . . ." There is obviously no need to separate these "from . . . to" clauses with a comma.

A comma should be used, however, to separate major clauses that are linked by conjunctions such as "and," "but," and "or." Sentences with two clauses joined by "and" seem to present particular problems to many writers. The writer must be careful to look at the intended meaning of his sentence to determine whether a comma is needed to warn the reader that a new idea is being introduced or whether a comma is not needed because no new idea is presented.

[C] Correct
Moreover, Omnicare operates within a broad cross-section of the health care industry, and all of its businesses are relatively recession-resistant.

In this case a comma is needed because the two clauses are independent clauses—they each can stand on their own. This sentence enumerates the attractive qualities of Omnicare, one of which is its operation within a cross-section of the health care industry. Another of these qualities is the resistance to recession of its businesses. It is widely accepted that writers may drop the comma, even when it is technically proper to include a comma, if the two clauses are quite short. We think such a practice is fine, but we must warn writers to be sure that the comma's elimination does not make the sentence difficult to comprehend.

Another important—and common—use of commas is to separate items in a series. In most instances the average writer's use of commas in such situations does not cause problems for the reader. There is, however, a common problem that, in fact, seems to be on the rise. This is the confusion created when writers habitually drop the final comma in a series such as: a, b, and c. The potential confusion this creates is reflected in Challenge D. The corrected version below eliminates this problem:

[D] Correct
After the acquisition, the company will be involved in three businesses: first aid supplies, janitor supplies and cleaning equipment, and safety equipment.

In the Challenge sentence as punctuated on page 95, it is difficult to determine exactly what the three businesses are. Are these the three businesses?

- first aid supplies
- janitor supplies and cleaning equipment
- safety equipment

Or are these the three businesses?

- first aid supplies
- janitor supplies
- cleaning equipment and safety equipment

The addition of the comma solves this problem immediately.

The Semicolon: Big Brother of the Comma;
Weak Sister of the Period

Challenge A
Most experts project a strong economy, however, we remain cautious.

> Economics staff member of a major corporation

Challenge B
During 1983, we plan to add approximately 200 new floral shops, 150 health foods departments, 130 service seafood shops and a like number of service meat counters plus about 120 in-store bakeries, 90 new delis and 80 cheese shops.

> The Kroger Co. 1982 annual report

Challenge C
The New England states will have 14 salespeople, the Mid-Atlantic, 6, the Southeast, 8, the Northwest, 4...

> A national sales manager, in his business plan

Make the appropriate corrections and read Review 29 to see how you did.

The Semicolon: Big Brother of the Comma; Weak Sister of the Period

In most cases you have three choices of punctuation when separating two independent clauses (independent means "able to stand on its own"): the period, the comma/conjunction combination, or the semicolon. The three "separating" forms of punctuation are shown below, as applied to sentences containing two independent clauses.

Sales in 1984 were up, and profits were down.

Sales in 1984 were up. Profits were down.

Sales in 1984 were up; profits were down.

None of the sentences above are wrong; the decision of which one to use depends on the strength of the break you want. As the title of this lesson intimates, the semicolon should be used when the break in the sentence is stronger than that provided by a comma but weaker than that provided by a period. Generally, such a situation arises when the two independent clauses are closely linked in meaning. Overall, the semicolon can be an excellent tool because it provides transition without being wordy.

Using the guidelines above, let's analyze Challenge A. Challenge A is wrong as is because none of the separating forms of punctuation discussed above are used to connect the two independent clauses. Rather, a comma—*without* the conjunction—is used ("however" is *not* a conjunction), and the comma is not strong enough by itself to effectively separate two independent clauses. The result is a "run-on" sentence. To correct Challenge A, then, we must decide precisely which type of separating punctuation we should use. (But first, if we may, let's place the "however" *after* the "we" for purposes of correct emphasis—refer to "Placement, However, Is Difficult," page 88.) Because the ideas expressed in the two clauses are closely linked—one contrasting with the other—we feel a period would be too strong. A comma-conjunction combination, on the other hand, not only would be awkward-sounding, but would be too weak a transition between the two ideas. A semicolon would provide just the right degree of separation while still allowing the reader to keep the ideas together in his mind.

[A] Correct and Preferred
Most experts project a strong economy; we, however, remain cautious.

Semicolons are also used to provide the separation needed when the various components of a series are long and/or contain commas. Challenge B is such a case (note the phrase beginning with "130" and ending with "bakeries"); unfortunately, no semicolons are provided, which makes for hazardous reading. We prefer the following version.

[B] Preferred
During 1983, we plan to add approximately 200 new floral shops; 150 health foods departments; 130 service seafood shops and a like number of service meat counters; 120 in-store bakeries; 90 new delis; and 80 cheese shops.

Challenge C illustrates another "series" problem, one that is especially common in business writing. When data and words are mixed in a series, as is done in Challenge C, semicolons are needed to eliminate confusion about which number corresponds to which region. Unfortunately, writers who are uncertain as to how to punctuate such a series will often resort to charts that are really not needed. The corrected version of Challenge C is shown below.

[C] Preferred
The New England states will have 14 salespeople; the Mid-Atlantic, 6; the Southeast, 8; the Northwest, 4 . . .

Parenthetical Punctuation

Challenge A
Throughout its history Betz has benefited from the growth of the hydrocarbon, paper, and primary metals industries, its major market areas, as well as industry in general.

Betz Laboratories 1983 annual report

Challenge B
The three key product groups, wafers, cakes, and egg cookies, further strengthened their leading market positions.

The Pillsbury Company 1982 annual report

Challenge C
Other forms of government intervention - import quotas and tariffs - have added to the inefficiencies of the market.

Letter from CEO of Fortune 500 company, as typed by secretary

Make the appropriate corrections and read Review 30 to see how you did.

Parenthetical Punctuation

Many sentences contain words or clauses that give examples or further information about the subject of the sentence but that are not necessary for the reader to understand the sentence. It may be important to relate this type of information to the reader, but it is also important not to distract him from the main purpose of the sentence. This information is normally referred to as parenthetical information, and, despite its name, it is usually set off from the main flow of the sentence by commas. There are instances, however, where commas are not the best choice. For example, the use of commas can be confusing in those cases where the sentence already contains a number of commas or in those cases where the parenthetical information itself contains a comma. This is where dashes and parentheses are helpful. Challenge A is an example of a sentence where the use of commas is a problem. A corrected version is shown below:

[A] Correct
Throughout its history Betz has benefited from the growth of the hydrocarbon, paper, and primary metals industries (its major market areas) as well as industry in general.

Also Correct
Throughout its history Betz has benefited from the growth of the hydrocarbon, paper, and primary metals industries—its major market areas—as well as industry in general.

The fact that either of the above versions is correct highlights another issue with regard to parenthetical phrases. Commas, dashes, and parentheses each convey a different message to the reader about the parenthetical information. Commas are neutral and give the parenthetical phrase about the same "weight" as the rest of the sentence. Parentheses tend to de-emphasize the parenthetical phrase, making it even more "parenthetical," if you will. Dashes, on the other hand, tend to emphasize the parenthetical phrase, calling attention to it. Consequently, either of the two versions of Challenge A shown above is correct; the writer, however, must choose which is more appropriate for his purposes.

The good business writer should be aware that many grammar "experts" feel that dashes are vastly overused. Their opinion is that the dash is a piece of punctuation that should be reserved for unusual situations. Although they may be correct about the overuse of dashes in journalistic and other popular writing, it has been our experience in business writing that dashes are very seldom used. We almost certainly have a more "liberal" opinion of the proper uses of dashes than do some of these experts; nonetheless, we are sure that most business writers can use dashes considerably more often than they now do without "overusing" them.

Below is the corrected version of Challenge B, which shows an effective use of dashes:

[B] Correct
The three key product groups—wafers, cakes, and egg cookies—further strengthened their leading market positions.

Although it might be argued that parentheses would have been effective, we feel that in a forum such as an annual report, the reader probably does not know what the three key product groups are and that this information is at least as important as the rest of the sentence. To put the three items in parentheses would have de-emphasized them—certainly not a crime, but not the true intent of the writer either. To leave the sentence as it originally was, however, *is* a crime. In fact, after our first reading of the original Challenge B, we thought there were *six* product groups—the three *key* product groups as well as wafers, cakes, and egg cookies—that strengthened their leading market positions.

Challenge C shows punctuation that has been used correctly but presented incorrectly. Dashes are represented in typed text by two hyphens typed together with no spaces following the preceding word and no spaces preceding the following word. The corrected "typed" (vs. typeset) version of Challenge C is shown below:

[C] Correct
Other forms of government intervention--import quotas and tariffs--have added to the inefficiencies of the market.

Hyphenate to Communicate

Challenge A
Division A has year to date net sales of . . .
> Monthly report of a corporate
> operating division

Challenge B
In the year to date, Division B has net sales of . . .
> Monthly report of a corporate
> operating division

Challenge C
I also served as cochairman of the company's United Appeal campaign.
> Résumé

Challenge D
We need to reform the task force to address the newly raised issue.
> Memo from task force leader of
> Fortune 500 company

Challenge E
Delivery will take from 15–20 days.
> Printed note from a major mail-
> order firm

Make the appropriate corrections and read Review 31 to see how you did.

Hyphenate to Communicate

We are all familiar with the use of a hyphen to divide a word that will not fit at the end of a line. Few of us, however, are familiar enough with the other uses of hyphens. Many of us have been taught to avoid the use of hyphens—taught that they belong only rarely in "proper" writing. Although we would agree that hyphens can easily be overused, there are a number of situations where the use of a hyphen is either necessary or helpful for the reader to comprehend what has been written.

The principal case where hyphens are an aid in comprehension is the joining of two or more words together to form a single, compound adjective (such as "high-powered"). Of course, some compound adjectives, such as "hardheaded," are used so often that they are now accepted as single words and can be found in most dictionaries. Other terms, such as *"laissez faire"* and "high school," are recognized as single ideas even though the words are not linked by hyphens. But there are many other compound terms that are used less often (or many times have just been "coined" by the writer) and are unclear without hyphens.

When uncertain whether or not to use a hyphen to join two words, refer to the following when-in-doubt rule: *Use a hyphen to join two or more words to form a compound adjective when there is any doubt as to meaning or when providing a hyphen makes the reader's task easier.* The only common exception to this rule is when the first word of the adjective phrase is an adverb ending in "-ly" (*e.g.,* "a completely clear conscience").

This when-in-doubt rule can be applied to Challenge A, the revised version of which is shown below:

[A] Correct
Division A has *year-to-date* net sales of . . .

Note that with hyphens, the words "year," "to," and "date" are combined to form a single adjective, making the sentence easier to read.

Challenge B, while a near mirror image of Challenge A, is *not* in need of hyphens. The phrase "year to date" has been repositioned in the sentence so that it is no longer a compound adjective and hyphenating it would not help the reader.

[B] Correct [No correction needed.]
In the year to date, Division B has net sales of . . .

Another case where hyphens aid in comprehension and readability is the joining of certain prefixes to nouns. "Co-" is an example of such a prefix, and the difficulty in reading a "co-" word that has no hyphen is illustrated by Challenge C. The correct version of Challenge C (shown below) separates "co" and "chairman" with a hyphen, helping the reader understand the word.

[C] Correct
I also served as *co-chairman* of the company's United Appeal campaign.

A third case where hyphens are needed, closely related to the prior case, is when the writer wishes to distinguish a little-used word or a word he is "coining" from another more common word. This can be seen in Challenge D.

[D] Correct
We need to *re-form* the task force to address the newly raised issue.

Although it is possible that the writer actually intended to use "reform" (to mean "improve"), we believe he meant "re-form" (to mean "form again").

A slightly different use of the hyphen is to indicate a range: "Delivery will take 15–20 days." In such a case, the hyphen is used in the place of "from...to," as in: "Delivery will take from 15 to 20 days." Do not, however, use a hyphen to replace the "to" alone in a "from...to" phrase, as Challenge E does. The corrected versions of Challenge E are shown below:

[E] Correct
Delivery will take *15–20* days.

Also Correct
Delivery will take *from 15 to 20* days.

The Magic Spell

Challenge A
This type of thing has been occuring for many years now.

> Chairman of a Fortune 500 company, in a memo to the president of a Fortune 100 company

Make the appropriate correction and read Review 32 to see how you did.

The Magic Spell

[A] Correct
This type of thing has been *occurring* for many years now.

"Occurring" has two "r's," as listed in *Webster's New World Dictionary, Second College Edition.*

"Occurring" is misspelled frequently; but, then again, so are many other words (including "misspelled"). It would do little good to attempt to list them all here, but we do feel that some advice is in order: Get in the habit of referring (two "r's," not one) to a dictionary *whenever* you have the *slightest* doubt as to the correct spelling of a word. A spelling error is unforgivable (no "e" between the "v" and the "a").

Also use the dictionary if you have the feeling that the word in question may be slang or a colloquial term (dictionaries assign usage labels to words). Such words should be used only for emphasis or for humor in business writing (and when used, they should typically be placed within quotation marks). These types of words can also be used occasionally (two "c's" and one "s") in more informal business communication.

Relatively Redundant

Challenge A

Recently, we have noticed a shift in the ratio of fixed compensation as a percent of total compensation.

> General manager, medium-size company

Challenge B

Company R's P/E is currently 8.5 times earnings.

> Analyst at a regional stock brokerage firm

Make the appropriate corrections and read Review 33 to see how you did.

Relatively Redundant

A ratio shows the size or number of one thing relative to the size or number of another: "The ratio of students to teachers is 24 to 1 [or 24:1]." A percent figure also indicates the size or number of one thing relative to another, but it is always expressed in terms of hundredths. Don't confuse the two words, and more important, don't use the two words in the same sentence, as is done in Challenge A. Challenge A should be revised in one of the following two ways:

[A] Correct
Recently, we have noticed a shift in the ratio of fixed compensation *to* total compensation.

Also Correct
Recently, we have noticed a shift *in fixed compensation expressed as a percent of total compensation.*

"P/E" is an abbreviation for "price-earnings ratio," or, alternatively, "price-earnings multiple." It represents the market price of a company's stock divided by the annual earnings-per-share figure. A P/E figure is conventionally expressed in one of two ways: (1) as a figure followed by an "X" ("8.5X" read "8.5 times") or (2) as a stand-alone figure ("8.5"). To express a P/E figure as "8.5 times earnings," as is done in Challenge B, is imprecise and redundant (it is the *price* that is 8.5 times earnings, not the price-earnings multiple).

[B] Correct
Company R's P/E is currently *8.5 [or 8.5X].*

Also Correct
Company R is *currently selling at* 8.5 times earnings.

Passive vs. Active Voice

Challenge A
A milestone in the Company's history was reached in May, 1982, when the Board of Directors declared the Company's first cash dividend.

> United Bankers, Inc., 1982 annual report

Challenge B
It is our expectation that through additional acquisitions, we will construct a network of companies that can operate first on a national and then on an international basis. Initiatives have been taken to penetrate the mining industry in the United States. New approaches are being taken to sell Quaker products for use on oil rigs that are engaged in drilling. We are actively exploring avenues to increase sales in the Soviet Union. Major emphasis will be placed, in 1984, on exploring and establishing a basis for serving the steel industry in India and the Peoples Republic of China.

> Quaker Chemical Corporation
> 1983 annual report

Make the appropriate corrections and read Review 34 to see how you did.

Passive vs. Active Voice

Active voice ("We did it") is much more vigorous and lively than passive voice ("It was done by us"). It is also more concise. In business writing, we recommend the use of active voice in most instances. The writer who uses the active voice appears more forceful and promotes a greater sense of confidence than the writer using the passive voice. Also, people tend to believe more in an active-voice statement than in a passive-voice statement. Let's now review the Challenge statements.

Challenge A is an excellent example of the passive voice taking all the punch out of what should be a powerful message. The company reached a milestone, goshdarnit...why don't they say it with some oomph (especially in an annual report)?

[A] Recommended
We reached [or "the Company reached"] a milestone in May, 1982, when the Board of Directors declared the Company's first cash dividend.

(*Note:* The phrase "in the Company's history" is unnecessary; it is implied by use of the word "milestone.")

As for Challenge B, four of the five sentences are written in passive voice. Notice how much more forceful and believable the paragraph is when the active voice predominates:

[B] Recommended
We plan to create, through additional acquisitions, a network of companies that can operate first on a national and then on an international basis. We have taken initiatives to penetrate the mining industry in the United States; we have adopted approaches to sell Quaker products for use on oil rigs that are engaged in drilling; we are actively exploring avenues to increase sales in

the Soviet Union; and we will place, in 1984, a major emphasis on exploring and establishing a basis for serving the steel industry in India and in the Peoples Republic of China.

There are times, however, when the use of passive voice should be considered. For example, the passive voice can be particularly purposeful when you are not willing to put your personal opinion on the line, as in the following sentence:

It is recommended [rather than "We recommend"] that the passive voice be used in such a case.

Odds and (Year) Ends

Challenge A
Exhibit XI sets forth the detailed income statement for the fiscal years ending September 20, 1981, 1982, and 1983.

> A research report by Rotan-Mosle, an investment bank in Houston, Texas, March 1984

Challenge B
I am not going to do it, irregardless of what you say.

> A common expression

Challenge C
Loan me the money.

> An even more common expression

Challenge D
I was late because I had to travel further than he.

> CPA at a Big Eight accounting firm

Challenge E
The analyst didn't say it outright, but he inferred that the acquisition was off.

> Stockbroker

Challenge F
All personnel in the sales organization are renumerated on a straight-salary basis.

> Report by Goldman, Sachs & Co., December 1984

Challenge G

I don't know about you, but I'm adverse to the entire marketing plan.

> Assistant to the president of a
> mid-size corporation

Make the appropriate corrections and read Review 35 to see how you did.

Odds and (Year) Ends

The Challenge statements on the previous pages represent the "odds and ends" of commonly committed business errors.

Use the phrase "years ended" when the years that you're speaking of *have ended*. "Years ending" is best used for future years.

[A] Correct
Exhibit XI sets forth the detailed income statement for the fiscal years *ended* September 30, 1981, 1982, and 1983.

"Irregardless" is listed in *Webster's New World Dictionary* as a "substandard redundancy for regardless." "Substandard," in our book, means "do not use it except for purposes of humor."

[B] Correct
I am not going to do it, *regardless* of what you say.

Avoid using "loan" as a verb. Use "lend" instead.

[C] Preferred
Lend me the money.

"Further" is another one of those words (much like the word "myself") that somehow developed the reputation of being "refined." Thus, we continually find the word creeping into people's everyday language, whether "further" or "*farther*" is truly meant. Here's the distinction:

Use "farther" only when dealing with actual distances (note the revised version of Challenge D below):

[D] Preferred
I was late because I had to travel *farther* than he.

Use "further" when dealing with concepts of time, degree, or quantity:

He developed the strategy further [*i.e.,* to a greater degree].

"Imply" means to indicate or suggest. "Infer" means to conclude or derive from certain evidence. As a rule, remember that the writer "implies" and the reader "infers." So, "infer" should generally be used in conjunction with the word "from," followed by the evidence.

[E] Correct
The analyst didn't say it outright, but he *implied* that the acquisition was off.

Also Correct
I *inferred* from the analyst's statements that the acquisition was off.

Regarding Challenge statements F and G, "renumeration" and "adverse" are so often used incorrectly in the place of "remuneration" and "averse," respectively, they deserve special mention in this lesson of odds and ends.

"Remunerate" means "to pay or compensate a person for work or service done." As for "renumerate," the word doesn't even exist in *Webster's New World Dictionary,* though there is an entry for "numerate"—it means "to enumerate." While one could argue that to renumerate means to (e)numerate once again, the word is used incorrectly in Challenge F.

[F] Correct
All personnel...are *remunerated* on a straight-salary basis.

"Averse" means "opposed (to); reluctant." "Adverse," on the other hand, means "unfavorable or harmful," as in "adverse effects of the recession."

[G] Correct
I don't know about you, but I'm *averse* to the entire marketing plan.

Credibility Checks

Challenge A
As the world emerged from WW II, heavy industry in the U.S. was dominant; intact, technically superior, and of impressive dimension.

> Betz Laboratories 1983 annual report

Challenge B
Particularly has this been beneficial in the corporate market where we have seen a marked increase in loan participations and loan syndications.

> First Interstate Bancorp 1982 annual report

Challenge C
Omnicare's HPI Health Care Services, Inc., which pioneered the use of the Unit Dose Drug Distribution System and the Intravenous (IV) Admixture System, added 19 new pharmacies during the year, managing pharmacies in 133 hospitals at the end of 1982, a 32% share of all contract pharmacies nationwide.

> Omnicare, Inc., 1982 annual report

Challenge D
Marketing is handled by 44 full-time salespeople based at each operating location.

> Rotan-Mosle, an investment bank in Houston, Texas

Make the appropriate corrections and read Review 36 to see how you did.

Credibility Checks

As a communicator in the business world, your most essential asset is credibility. Without credibility, your message drowns in a sea of doubt. Errors in logic, composition, and grammar (especially obvious ones) all tend to chip away at your credibility. Thus it is critical to thoroughly check your work.

Thoroughly checking your work is painstaking. Time permitting, your piece of communication should be read through at least twice. Below are listed the three primary areas that should be reviewed when checking.

1. The Readability. Are sentences crisp, clear? Are there any nuts-and-bolts errors (spelling, grammar, punctuation)? Are transitions smooth and effective?

2. The Audience. Put yourself in the place of the primary audience (*i.e.,* the intended recipients): Is the tone correct? Is the language too technical? At the same time, keep the secondary audience (*i.e.,* the "others" who may get their hands on your document) in mind: Are the tone and language appropriate for them also?

3. The Message. Does it say what you intend it to say? Is the "bottom line" clear? Is it adequately supported? Is the logic tight?

We suggest strongly that, when possible, sufficient time separate the writing of the document and the checking of the document. One or two hours will do, but "sleeping on it" for a night is preferred. Also, put physical distance between yourself and the paper when checking your work—try standing up, arms extended . . . it works. Last, read the piece aloud at least once. Let your ears participate. Hear how it sounds. As Professor Paul W. Schwartz of the Harvard Business School puts it in his course on Management Communication: "A complicity of eye and ear does wonders toward picking out the flaws, firming up the essential transitions, and detecting those inductive leaps."

Now for the Challenge statements. Yes, we can hardly believe it either. . . . These four statements, three of which were printed in annual reports, bear no evidence that they were checked.

The phrase "of impressive dimension" in Challenge A not only borders on being non-parallel (refer to "Perilous Non-Parallels," page 65), but also seems to be a long-winded way of saying "massive." In addition, the semicolon in Challenge A is incorrect (refer to "The Semicolon: Big Brother of the Comma; Weak Sister of the Period," page 99). Because of this incorrect use of the semicolon, we aren't certain what Betz intended to say, but here are two possible correct revisions:

[A] Correct
As the world emerged from WW II, heavy industry in the U.S. was dominant: it was massive; it was intact; and it was technically superior.

Also Correct
As the world emerged from WW II, heavy industry in the U.S. was dominant inasmuch as it was massive, intact, and technically superior.

First Interstate should have read Challenge B *aloud* . . . at a board meeting, perhaps. This sentence should never have made it into print. Who would ever say, "Particularly has this been beneficial"?

[B] Recommended
This has been particularly beneficial . . .

We can hardly make heads or tails of Challenge C, but here is an attempt to "fine-tune" the statement.

[C] Recommended
Omnicare's HPI Health Care Services, Inc., which pioneered

the use of the Unit Dose Drug Distribution System and the Intravenous (IV) Admixture System, added 19 new pharmacies during the year. At the end of 1982, the division was managing pharmacies in 133 hospitals, a level representing a 32% share of all contract pharmacies nationwide.

As Challenge D now reads, there seem to be 44 full-time salespeople at *each* location. That's a lot of salespeople. Of course, Rotan-Mosle meant to say that there are 44 full-time salespeople, *total,* and that there is at least one of these salespeople at each location. One other suggestion for this sentence: It should be written in active voice.

[D] Recommended
Forty-four full-time salespeople, at least one at each location, handle the marketing [distribution?] function.

Also Recommended
Forty-four full-time salespeople handle the marketing function.

(*Note:* We recommend this version only if the fact that there is at least one salesperson at each location is deemed insignificant.)

II
GOOD
GRAPHS
AT A
GLANCE

INTRODUCTION

Numbers and graphic devices play a major role in almost all business reports, memos, letters, and presentations. Not only do they clarify verbal material and present data that would be cumbersome to explain verbally, they also add spice and increase reader interest. If effectively presented, in fact, the numbers and graphic devices in a report can be the heart of the message.

So, just as the packaging of words is crucial in verbal communications, the packaging of *data and graphics* is crucial in *"non-verbal" communications*. But the packaging of data and graphics is a highly specialized skill, one that few have mastered. No "set" rules exist, and very few books even broach the topic. And now, with the advent of the personal computer, the role of the chart in the business world has reached new heights. This "Good Graphs at a Glance" section—devoted to rules for the packaging and presentation of data and graphs in business communications—is specialized and comprehensive enough to fulfill the needs of today's business person.

THE RULES

Because no "set" body of rules for chart presentation currently exists, there is no "set" right and wrong. The single criterion we used in formulating the guidelines set forth in the following pages was: Does the technique in question enhance the clarity, the readability, and the logical presentation of charts?

In answering this question and in making the various determinations, we drew upon our experience in critically examining charts over the years. We both started our careers with Chemed, a subsidiary of W. R. Grace & Co. Grace is a company that strives, perhaps a mite harder than most companies, for precision and clarity in charts. After being indoctrinated in the Grace system, we both packed our bags for Harvard Business School, where every night's preparation required analyzing three cases, each with its fair share of charts. It was here that we learned frustration . . . and with it, we learned the importance of Grace's high level of chart standards. While most charts were clear and well organized at HBS, those that were not wasted time we didn't have. We started to understand what executives feel like when something (even a little thing) is unclear or inaccurate in a chart. There's no one around to ask, and no time to ask, anyway. The only difference is that, as students, we had to live with it and do the best we could. Executives can either have the chart replaced . . . or have the creator replaced.

After business school, we both returned to Chemed with our chart consciousnesses raised and began formulating our own set of rules for effective chart presentation. As with the grammar section, we narrowed our list of rules to only those that business people at large have the most difficulty with. And, once again, such a task involved screening a multitude of works from a multitude of sources and weighing the various "errors" according to the source.

As it turned out, the preponderance of chart-related errors was found in *tables* rather than in *graphic charts* (the distinction is defined on page 131). Consequently, you will find in this section a bias in favor of tables. But, if you happen to personally favor graphic charts, do not despair: Most of the table-related rules also apply to the graphic charts; moreover, the final lesson gives helpful pointers on each of the popular graphic chart forms.

THE FORMAT

We have been able to carry over into this graphs section the challenge-then-review format used in the grammar section. Instead of dedicating an entire challenge-then-review lesson to each rule, though, we have combined—for reasons of efficiency— several rules per lesson. In order to combine rules in an organized and logical fashion, we constructed charts that contained the selected combination of problem areas. Thus, the Challenge charts in this section have not been (and cannot be) attributed to anyone in particular.

For easy reference, a summary of *all* the chart-related rules has been included as the final section in "Good Graphs at a Glance."

Selection of a Chart Form

Challenge A
There are only a couple of different types of chart forms that can be used to present data.

Challenge B
It doesn't matter which chart form you select.

Examine and comment on the content of the two Challenges. Read the Introductory Review for the "answers."

Selection of a Chart Form

[A] Comment

Challenge A is inaccurate because, in fact, there are several different chart forms that can be used to present data. The *tabular chart* (*i.e.*, the *table*) presents data separated into columns and rows and is the most common of chart forms. Tables can demonstrate five or more relationships at once and thus are best suited for presenting a "multi-dimensional" story. The other chart forms can all be classified as *graphic charts,* for they each use one or more of the following graphic devices to *represent* data (versus tables, which *present* data): columns (used in *bar charts*), lines (used in *line/curve graphs*), pies (used in *pie charts*), dots (used in *correlation charts* and *position charts*), maps (used in *geographical charts*), and pictures (used in *pictograms*). In contrast with tables, graphic charts typically focus on and highlight a *single* relationship. To illustrate, a table can show an entire balance sheet—assets, liabilities, stockholders' equity, and the components of each—for a period of ten years or more. A graphic chart, on the other hand, can pinpoint only, say, total assets, and show them for ten or more years. (Alternatively, the graphic chart can show the mix of the various balance sheet components, but for only one year.) Because of this, use caution when presenting graphic charts, for the data you are representing will generally have been taken "out of context."

[B] Comment

Challenge B is inaccurate because it *does* matter which chart form you select. Different chart forms are appropriate in different situations, depending on your objective. If you wish to demonstrate several relationships at once or to show a "complete picture," the table is for you. If, however, you would like to focus on one or two relationships or dimensions, the graphic chart is generally appropriate (though a table is hardly ever inappropriate). The specific *type* of graphic chart you select depends on the *type(s)* of relationship(s) you wish to demonstrate. Described in the Introductory Exhibits are the eight basic types of relationships and the corresponding chart form or forms that are appropriate for each one. (Remember that tables can also be used to demonstrate most of these types of relationships.)

INTRODUCTORY EXHIBIT A

Type of Relationship	Relationship Type Defined	Real-World Example
TIME SERIES COMPARISON	Shows variation over time	Sales of Company A from 1980 to 1985

Appropriate Chart Forms

1. BAR CHART

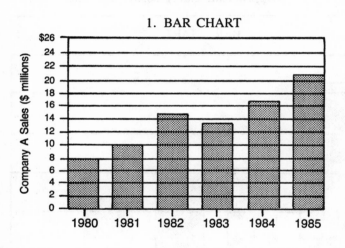

2. LINE GRAPH

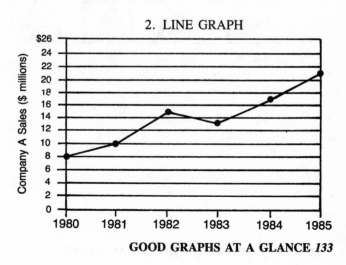

Type of Relationship	Relationship Type Defined	Real-World Example
RANKING	Ranks items according to size, impact, degree, etc.	The top five companies in the industry

Appropriate Chart Form

BAR CHART

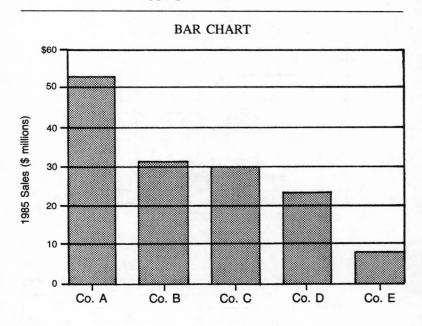

INTRODUCTORY EXHIBIT C

Type of Relationship	Relationship Type Defined	Real-World Example
PARTS OF A WHOLE	Shows the relative size of the various parts of the whole	Business segments of Company X

Appropriate Chart Forms

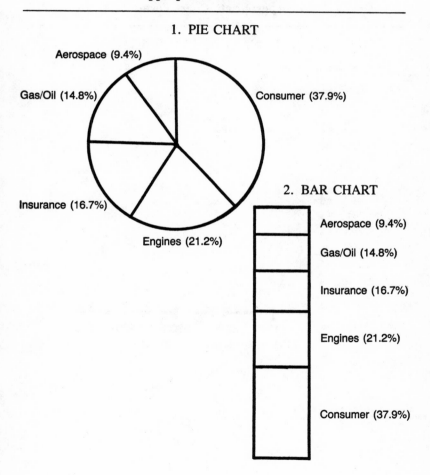

1. PIE CHART

Aerospace (9.4%)

Gas/Oil (14.8%)

Consumer (37.9%)

Insurance (16.7%)

Engines (21.2%)

2. BAR CHART

Aerospace (9.4%)

Gas/Oil (14.8%)

Insurance (16.7%)

Engines (21.2%)

Consumer (37.9%)

INTRODUCTORY EXHIBIT D

Type of Relationship	Relationship Type Defined	Real-World Example
CORRELATION	Shows how a change in one set of data affects a second set of data	Relationship between size of firm in the industry and operating margin

Appropriate Chart Form

DOT CHART (or XY CHART)

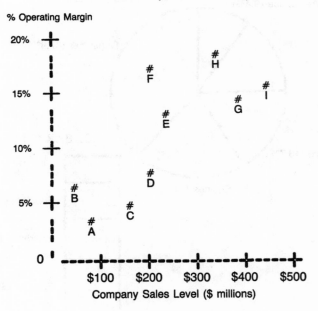

% Operating Margin

20%

#
H

#
F

15%
#
G   #
I

#
E

10%

#
D

#
B
5%
#
C

#
A

0

$100 $200 $300 $400 $500

Company Sales Level ($ millions)

Type of Relationship	Relationship Type Defined	Real-World Example
FREQUENCY DISTRIBUTION	Shows frequency of distribution among certain intervals	Experience mix of a sales force

Appropriate Chart Forms

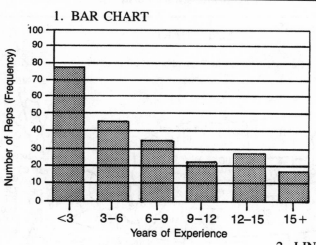

1. BAR CHART

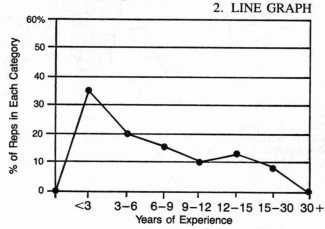

2. LINE GRAPH

INTRODUCTORY EXHIBIT F

Type of Relationship	Relationship Type Defined	Real-World Example
GEOGRAPHICAL	Shows how geographical regions compare with each other	1980–2000 projected population growth by state

Appropriate Chart Form

MAP CHART

Percent Change in Population, 1980 to 2000

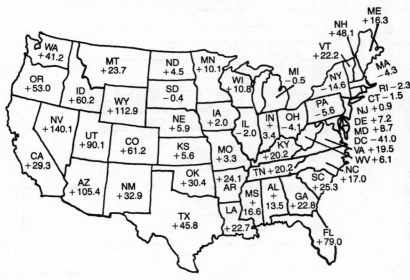

Alaska +57.5%
Hawaii +32.4%
Washington, D.C. −41%
U.S. +18.1%

Source: Census Bureau

Type of Relationship	Relationship Type Defined	Real-World Example
FLOW	Shows the flow of materials or processes (= a "flow chart") or shows the "flow" of reporting relationships (= an "organizational chart")	The flow chart for capital appropriation requests or the organizational chart for Company Q

Appropriate Chart Forms

1. FLOW CHART

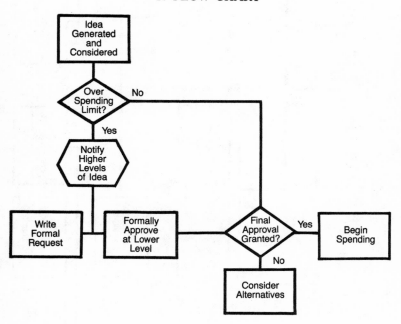

2. ORGANIZATIONAL CHART

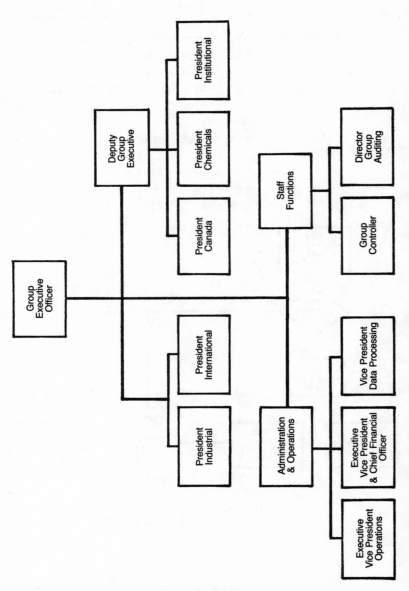

Type of Relationship	Relationship Type Defined	Real-World Example
INDUSTRY POSITION	Shows a two-dimensional comparison among competitors (or products) in an industry.*	Price/Image positioning of bath care products

Appropriate Chart Form

POSITIONING CHART

Bath Product Price/Image Positions**

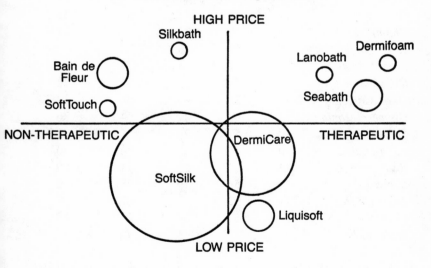

*The dimensions selected should be the two most strategically significant dimensions (e.g., in the beer market, a positioning chart might "position" companies along the price dimension and the age-of-the-target-market dimension).
**Size of bubble represents dollar share.

The Important Cosmetics, Part I

The Lead-in
The following exhibit provides a user profile of major skin care products in the hand and body segment.

BRAND	AGE BREAKDOWN OF BRAND USERS			INCOME BREAKDOWN OF BRAND USERS	
	18–24	**25–45**	**46+**	**<$25K**	**>$25K**
Liquisoft	16%	40%	44%	64%	36%
Opaque	14	55	31	65	35
Chantilles	18	46	37	72	28
Terra-Lotion	21	56	23	72	28
Body Smooth	19	53	28	75	25
Oil of Manet	13	54	33	72	28
DermiCare	27	54	19	68	32
Creme d'Monique	15	64	21	64	36
SoftSilk	19	52	29	64	35
Lano-cream	20	55	25	70	30
R&R Baby Oil	23	52	25	71	29
Supra Gel	25	56	19	68	32
Jojoba Gelee	11	52	37	62	38
L'Aapres	12	54	34	61	39
Dermifoam	12	42	46	72	28

Make the appropriate improvements and read Review 1 for the answers.

The Important Cosmetics, Part I

The title. Always provide a title for your chart (even a chart that has an effective "lead-in"). A chart without a title is like a book without a title. The title is the first thing that most people read, and, if chosen carefully, the title gives the readers a meaningful entree to the "textless" story you are about to tell them. In addition, a reader scanning a report may look only at the charts and not read the text, making the title crucial.

Your title should be fairly complete. Tell not only what you are showing or what you are comparing, but over what time period your data applies (*e.g.*, "1974–1984" or "1982–1984 by Quarters") and/or what unit of measure is being used (*e.g.*, "$000's" to denote thousands or "millions of 1983 dollars" to denote millions of constant dollars with 1983 as the constant or base year). This unit-of-measure information is best located below the underscore of the title as illustrated:

Division XYZ vs. Competitor ABC
Net Sales and Gross Profit
1980–1984 by Quarters

($ millions)

As for the Challenge chart, we recommend the following title:

1981 Age and Income Profiles of
Users of Hand and Body Skin Care Products

Numbering rows and columns. How many times have you heard someone, typically in a meeting, refer to a number in a chart with a comment like this one: "I have a question about the figure in the . . . two . . . four . . . six . . . eight . . . *ninth* column and . . . oh . . . about twelve . . . thirteen, maybe fourteen lines

GOOD GRAPHS AT A GLANCE *143*

down"? A bit tedious, no? Well, all such nonsense can be easily avoided by numbering both the rows and the columns. The end result is a clean, clear question such as, "I have a question about the number in row thirteen, column nine."

Source. When it is not obvious, include the source of the data in the chart, either by using footnotes or by simply writing "Source: ———" at the bottom of the chart.

Spacing. To make the data more readable, break the rows, every four or five lines, with a space. (Doing this also makes the chart look clean.) In some cases, there will be a logical place for a break other than every fourth or fifth row. An example is the following "business-plan-type" chart format:

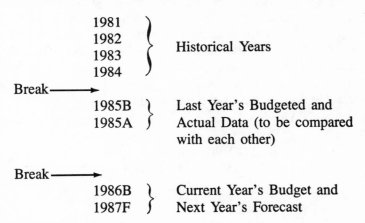

```
              1981  ⎞
              1982  ⎟
              1983  ⎬   Historical Years
              1984  ⎠
Break ────→
              1985B ⎱   Last Year's Budgeted and
              1985A ⎰   Actual Data (to be compared
                        with each other)

Break ────→
              1986B ⎱   Current Year's Budget and
              1987F ⎰   Next Year's Forecast
```

Another example involves months of the year: A natural grouping in such a case would be by quarter (January, February, March—April, May, June—July, August, September—October, November, December).

Numbering charts. Always consider numbering your charts. Such a practice makes for better organization and for easier reference (it's simpler to refer to "Chart 2" than "The chart on the following page"). You have a great deal of flexibility when numbering charts. You don't even have to refer to them as "charts"; "exhibits," "figures," "diagrams," and "tables" are all acceptable (but be consistent). In addition, although numbers are generally used to "number" charts, letters or a combination of numbers and letters (as we've used in this book) are both acceptable (but be consistent). Below, in Exhibit 1-A, we have shown the three acceptable methods of "numbering" charts.

EXHIBIT 1-A
THREE METHODS OF "NUMBERING" CHARTS

Numbers	Letters	Combination	
1	A	1	
2	B		
3	C		
.	.	2-A ⎫	grouped together
.	.	2-B ⎬	for a reason
.	.	2-C ⎭	
	AA		
	AB	3	
	AC	4	
	.		
	.	5-A ⎫	grouped together
	.	5-B ⎭	for a reason
	BA	.	
	BB	.	
	BC	.	
	.		
	.		
	.		

Generally, the chart number (or exhibit number, or table number, or whatever) should be included in two places:

1. In the lead-in: "Exhibit X provides a user profile..."

2. In the chart title:

EXHIBIT X
1981 Age and Income Profiles of
Users of Hand and Body Skin Care Products

Exhibit 1-B presents Challenge Chart 1 after the improvements suggested above have been incorporated.

(Exhibit follows on next page.)

EXHIBIT 1-B
CHALLENGE CHART 1 REVISED

The Lead-in:

User profiles of major skin care products in the hand and body segment are shown in Exhibit X.

EXHIBIT X
1981 Age and Income Profiles of
Users of Hand and Body Skin Care Products

	(1)	(2)	(3)	(4)	(5)
					INCOME
	AGE BREAKDOWN OF BRAND USERS			BREAKDOWN OF BRAND USERS	
BRAND	**18–24**	**25–45**	**46 +**	**<$25K**	**>$25K**
(1) *Liquisoft*	16%	40%	44%	64%	36%
(2) *Opaque*	14	55	31	65	35
(3) *Chantilles*	18	46	37	72	28
(4) *Terra-Lotion*	21	56	23	72	28
(5) *Body Smooth*	19	53	28	75	25
(6) *Oil of Manet*	13	54	33	72	28
(7) *DermiCare*	27	54	19	68	32
(8) *Creme d'Monique*	15	64	21	64	36
(9) *SoftSilk*	19	52	29	64	35
(10) *Lano-cream*	20	55	25	70	30
(11) *R&R Baby Oil*	23	52	25	71	29
(12) *Supra Gel*	25	56	19	68	32
(13) *Jojoba Gelee*	11	52	37	62	38
(14) *L'Aapres*	12	54	34	61	39
(15) *Dermifoam*	12	42	46	72	28

Source: The Voet Report, 1981

The Important Cosmetics, Part II

The Lead-in

[This chart was the initial part of a major section in a report. Discussion relating to the chart immediately followed the chart, but no lead-in was provided.]

EXHIBIT X
QUIMBY Company
Profit and Loss Statement
1984 Actual vs. 1984 Budget

($000)

	(1)	(2)	(3)	(4)	(5)
			% Inc./	% of Net Sales	
			(Dec.):		
	1984	1984	1984A vs.	1984	1984
	Budget	Actual	1984B	Budget	Actual
(1) Sales	$155	$166	7.1 %	100.0 %	100.0 %
(2) Cost of Sales	$63	$74	17.5 %	40.6 %	44.6 %
(3) Gross Margin	$92	$92	0.0 %	59.4 %	55.4 %
(4) Oper. Expense	$72	$71	(1.4)%	46.5 %	42.8 %
(5) Oper. Profit	$20	$21	5.0 %	12.9 %	12.6 %
(6) Other Inc/(Exp)	($2)	($3)	50.0 %	(1.3)%	(1.8)%
(7) Pretax Income	$18	$18	0.0 %	11.6 %	10.8 %
(8) Taxes	$9	$9	0.0 %	5.8 %	5.4 %
(9) Aftertax Income	$9	$9	0.0 %	5.8 %	5.4 %

Source: Variance Report

Make the appropriate improvements and read Review 2 for the answers.

The Important Cosmetics, Part II

The lead-in. Every chart needs some form of lead-in. Without such an introduction, the chart is in limbo and has no anchor to the rest of the document. In fact, the lead-in represents the first part of the following three-part, universal guide to communicating effectively (modified slightly to apply specifically to chart presentation): (1) Tell them what you are going to show them; (2) Show them; (3) Tell them what you have just shown them.

The lead-in need not be complex—a simple, one-line description of what the reader is about to see is usually sufficient. The following is an example of a lead-in you might use for the Challenge chart:

Exhibit X summarizes Quimby's 1984 performance as it compares with budget.

If Exhibit X is too large for the space remaining on the page, place the exhibit on the following page and include, as a part of the lead-in, a parenthetical expression indicating that the exhibit follows on the next page:

Exhibit X summarizes Quimby's 1984 performance as it compares with budget.

(Exhibit X follows on next page.)

In such a case, the text that is to follow the exhibit (*i.e.,* the text that tells them what you've just shown them) should go *after* the exhibit, even if there is room available at the bottom of the lead-in page. This rule may sound obvious, but it was included because some books recommend that all pages be "filled." (Please note that this rule has been violated here in our book, but only because to do so is publishing industry convention.)

Underscores. The single underscore should be used only when a column is being added or subtracted; never use the single underscore if a column *cannot* be added or subtracted. An example of a very common mistake exists in the Challenge chart. Each of the five columns can be subtracted vertically, *except column 3*. But since the underscores are present in column 3, the unsuspecting reader may think that the numbers *should* add. To prevent such potential confusion, leave underscores out of the column in such a case.

The *double* underscore, on the other hand, should be used only to denote *grand* totals. In the Challenge chart, double underscores are conspicuously and incorrectly absent in row 9, columns 1, 2, 4, and 5. (Row 9, column 3 should not have one because, once again, the number in that figure does not represent a total.)

Symbols. Symbols, such as dollar signs and percent signs, should not be repeated each row of a column as is done in the Challenge chart. By repeating the symbol, the author complicates the chart with unnecessary garble. The general rule is that a symbol should be used to begin each section or tier of data, and should be used with any number that is double-underscored (and with any number immediately *below* a double-underscored figure, for this represents, in effect, the beginning of a new section of data). The mini-table on page 151 illustrates this rule.

Favorable and unfavorable. Let's suppose it is your job to analyze why Quimby Company's aftertax profits were even with budget in a year when sales were up 7.1% from budget. Your instincts take you initially to column 3, but you quickly find that a number that is negative is not necessarily "bad" and one that is positive is not necessarily "good." Consequently, in order to determine whether the (positive) 17.5% figure in row 2 is good or bad, you must first check to see if it is associated with an income item (then it's good) or with an expense item (then it's bad). The same thing must then be done with all the other

Product Line	Sales	
Fasteners	$31	←——Beginning of section
Nuts	25	
Bolts	64	
Nails	71	
	———	
Total	$191	←——Double-underscored figure
	≡≡≡	
Memo: Export Sales	$47	←——Immediately below double-underscored figure

	As a % of Total	
Fasteners	16.2%	←——Beginning of new tier
Nuts	13.1	
Bolts	33.5	
Nails	37.2	
	———	
Total	100.0%	←——Double-underscored figure
	≡≡≡	
Memo: Export Sales	24.6%	←——Immediately below double-underscored figure

figures in column 3 in order to fully understand the chart. If, on the other hand, parentheses were used to indicate an *unfavorable variance*, rather than simply a decrease, and no parentheses were used to indicate a *favorable variance*, rather than simply an increase, the chart would be easier to scan—all negative numbers would be "bad" and all positive numbers "good." [*Note:* When cost of sales (or any other expense item) increases, it's an *unfavorable* variance; when it decreases, it's a *favorable* variance (the reverse is true in each case for the income items).]

While this hint is certainly helpful when it comes to profit-and-loss statements and to other types of charts, we would not recommend its use with balance sheets. The problem with the application of favorable/(unfavorable) to balance sheets is that if, say, inventories increase, is that good or bad? We all have our personal opinions on such an issue, but there is certainly no consensus.

Exhibit 2-A presents the Challenge chart after all the improvements recommended above have been made.

(Exhibit follows on next page.)

EXHIBIT 2-A
CHALLENGE CHART 2 REVISED

The Lead-in

Exhibit X summarizes Quimby's 1984 performance as it compares with budget.

EXHIBIT X
QUIMBY Company
Profit and Loss Statement
1984 Actual vs. 1984 Budget

($000)

	(1)	(2)	(3)	(4)	(5)
			% Var. Fav./ (Unfav.):	% of Net Sales	
	1984 Budget	1984 Actual	1984A vs. 1984B	1984 Budget	1984 Actual
(1) Sales	$155	$166	7.1 %	100.0 %	100.0 %
(2) Cost of Sales	63	74	(17.5)	40.6	44.6
(3) Gross Margin	92	92	0.0	59.4	55.4
(4) Oper. Expense	72	71	1.4	46.5	42.8
(5) Oper. Profit	20	21	5.0	12.9	12.6
(6) Other Inc/(Exp)	(2)	(3)	(50.0)	(1.3)	(1.8)
(7) Pretax Income	18	18	0.0	11.6	10.8
(8) Taxes	9	9	0.0	5.8	5.4
(9) Aftertax Income	$9	$9	0.0 %	5.8 %	5.4 %

Source: Variance Report

Structure, Part I

The Lead-in
Exhibit X highlights how funds have been expended in the Master's degree programs as compared with the other professional degree programs.

(Exhibit follows on next page.)

EXHIBIT X

Distribution of FY1964 Institutional Grant Expenditures by Use and by Class of Institution

Use of Institutional Grant Funds	(1) Total	(2) %	(3) I	(4) %	(5) II	(6) %	(7) III	(8) %
					Class of Institution(a)			
(1) TOTAL	$5,736,855	100%	$495,006	100%	$932,635	100%	$4,309,214	100%
(2) Computers	316,789	5.5	12,114	2.4	78,632	8.4	226,043	5.2
(3) Curricular Development	20,424	.35	1,839	.4	8,585	.9	10,000	0.2
(4) Equipment	2,028,389	35.4	318,932	64.4	406,804	43.6	1,302,653	30.2
(5) Facilities	293,236	5.1	37,605	7.6	50,725	5.4	204,906	4.8
(6) Faculty Research Proj	689,741	12.0	12,158	2.5	73,746	7.9	603,837	14.0
(7) Faculty Salaries	451,235	7.9	11,323	2.3	45,736	4.9	394,176	9.1
(8) Library Resources	391,595	6.8	24,681	5.0	35,393	3.8	331,521	7.7
(9) Miscellaneous	60,918	1.05	1,688	.3	9,935	1.1	49,295	1.1
(10) Student Stipends	202,310	3.5	9,220	1.9	26,331	2.8	166,759	3.9
(11) Travel	57,064	1	3,741	.7	9,249	1	44,074	1.0
(12) Untabulated	1,225,154	21.4	61,705	12.5	187,499	20	975,950	22.6
(13) Visiting Lecturers	45,354	.8	6,640	1.3	3,252	.3	35,462	0.8

(a) Institutional Class:
   I: Bachelor's and/or first professional degree
   II: Master's and/or second professional degree
   III: Ph.D. and equivalent degrees

Source: American Society for Engineering Education

Make the appropriate improvements and read Review 3 for the answers.

Structure, Part I

A good storyteller knows how to structure his story. There's always the easy way . . . and then there's the right way. The same holds true for structuring charts. By carelessly slapping together the important components of a chart, you could be significantly weakening your punch line. The hints on structuring that are included in these next two lessons should help ensure a knockout chart.

Column titles. Column titles should be fully descriptive, even if this means constructing a three-, four-, or five-line title. Footnotes are acceptable in a column title in order to indicate a source, to indicate reasons behind unusual trends in the column, or to indicate how the data were calculated; but to use a footnote to help *describe* the column data, as was done in the Challenge chart, is certainly awkward and potentially confusing for the reader.

We recommend the following column titles for the foregoing Challenge chart.

Institutional Class		
Class I: Bachelor's and First Professional Degrees	Class II: Master's and Second Professional Degrees	Class III: Ph.D. and Equivalent Degrees

Total column/row last. When listing components of a whole, always place the total last. This means that when you are summing numbers in a column, the total should appear at the *bottom* of the column (not at the top as is done in the Challenge chart); and when you are summing numbers in a row, the total should appear at the far right (not at the far left as is done in the Challenge chart). In this way, as the reader scans the page, he can mentally sum the components in a much easier and more natural fashion.

As an aside, when you show a total, don't ever leave out any component of the total. Grouping the least important components into an "Other" or "Miscellaneous" column or row is acceptable, but to require the reader to mentally derive any missing pieces by subtracting the given pieces from the total is not acceptable or wise.

Apples to apples. All data should be arranged so that comparable data are grouped together. In Challenge Chart 3, dollar figures are mixed with percentage figures; so, when comparing the percent data of Class I with those of Class II, the reader must cut across columns of dissimilar data. By doing this, the author of the chart has distracted the reader. Our recommendation, therefore, is the following structure (the two sections are, of course, to be placed side by side):

(1)	**(2)**	**(3)**	**(4)**
Expenditures by Class of Institution			
Class I: Bachelor's and First Professional Degrees	**Class II: Master's and Second Professional Degrees**	**Class III: Ph.D. and Equivalent Degrees**	**Total**

(5)	**(6)**	**(7)**	**(8)**
As a Percent of Respective Total			
Class I: Bachelor's and First Professional Degrees	**Class II: Master's and Second Professional Degrees**	**Class III: Ph.D. and Equivalent Degrees**	**Total**

Ordering data. When one presents income statement data (or balance sheet data), the ordering is easy. The sales data come first, then the cost of goods sold, and so on. But what about other types of charts, such as the Challenge chart, whose data cannot be packaged in such a standard format? Generally, the worst way to structure the data in such a case is on an alphabetical basis as is done in the Challenge chart. The best way is to order the data on the basis of a *ranking*. A baseball statistician, for example, might rank data according to the number of lifetime home runs; a Fortune 500 writer might rank data according to 1975–1985 average annual sales increase; and an economic analyst might rank data according to national debt as a percent of national GNP. The general rule, of course, is to rank based on either the most significant column of data or the column of data that you most want to highlight.

Concerning the Challenge chart specifically, given that the focus of the chart is Class II data (as indicated by the lead-in), probably the Class II data should be used to rank items. (The alternative is to rank the data in the total column, which would also be appropriate.) When you rank data, by the way, it is a good idea to indicate the ranked column by writing ''*Ranked*'' above the column title and the column number, as illustrated:

Chart Title

	Ranked	
(1)	**(2)**	**(3)**
Column	**Column**	**Column**
Title	**Title**	**Title**

Such a notation should eliminate any question in the reader's mind as to how you've ordered the data.

Significant digits. Always make a conscious decision as to the number of digits that are significant enough to be included in your chart. In other words, decide whether the data should be in billions, millions, or thousands. Too many digits is cumbersome; too few eliminates significant information.

The Challenge chart is an example of a chart whose data have too many digits. (Typically, when a majority of the numbers show five or more digits, there are too many.) The result is a crowded, messy appearance that distracts the reader. We recommend presenting the data in thousands of dollars. Please note that by "rounding off" the data in such a fashion, your columns/rows may not add. (In fact, it will likely occur in the percent columns/rows whether you round off or not.) In such a case, we recommend simply putting the following caveat at the bottom of the chart: Columns/rows may not add due to rounding.

Be consistent in the use of decimals. All numbers in a particular column (within a particular tier) should have the same number of digits to the right of the decimal—to do otherwise is distracting. In fact, all columns that are comparable with each other or that "flow" together should have a similar number of "decimal" digits.

The Challenge chart is in violation of the above decimal rule: Percentage figures in row 1, row 10, and row 13 have *no* decimal digits; percentage figures in rows 11 and 12 (column 2) have *two* decimal digits; and the rest of the percentage figures all have *one* decimal digit. Because all of the percentage figures in this chart are comparable, all should have the same number of decimal digits (preferably one).

In addition, numbers between 0 and 1 (like 0.8) should never be presented without the zero before the decimal. The figure in row 9, column 2 of the Challenge chart lacks such a zero (it is shown as ".8"), and other figures in columns 4 and 6 also lack the zero (they are shown as ".7," ".4," ".3," etc.)—one is not certain, in these cases, whether a non-zero number is missing or the zero was simply disregarded.

Exhibit 3-A presents the Challenge chart in its revised form (excluding the lead-in, which was appropriate).

(Exhibit follows on next page.)

EXHIBIT 3-A

CHALLENGE CHART 3 REVISED

EXHIBIT X

**Distribution of FY1964 Institutional Grant Expenditures
by Use and by Class of Institution**

($000)

	Ranked						
	(1)	(2)	(3)	(4)	(5)	(6)	(7)	(8)
	Expenditures by Class of Institution				As a Percent of Respective Total			
Use of Institutional Grant Funds	Class I: Bachelor's and First Professional Degrees	Class II: Master's and Second Professional Degrees	Class III: Ph.D. and Equivalent Degrees	Total	Class I: Bachelor's and First Professional Degrees	Class II: Master's Second and Professional Degrees	Class III: Ph.D. and Equivalent Degrees	Total
(1) Equipment	$318.9	$406.8	$1,302.7	$2,028.4	63.6%	43.5%	30.0%	35.1%
(2) Untabulated	61.7	187.5	976.0	1,225.2	12.3	20.0	22.5	21.2
(3) Computers	12.1	78.6	226.0	316.7	2.4	8.4	5.2	5.5
(4) Faculty Research Proj	12.2	73.7	603.8	689.7	2.4	7.9	13.9	11.9
(5) Facilities	37.6	50.7	204.9	293.2	7.5	5.4	4.7	5.1
(6) Faculty Salaries	11.3	45.7	394.2	451.2	2.3	4.9	9.1	7.8
(7) Library Resources	24.7	35.4	331.5	391.6	4.9	3.8	7.6	6.8
(8) Student Stipends	9.2	26.3	116.8	202.3	1.8	2.8	3.8	3.5
(9) Miscellaneous	1.7	9.9	49.3	60.9	0.3	1.1	1.1	1.1
(10) Travel	3.7	9.2	44.1	57.0	0.7	1.0	1.0	1.0

(11) Curricular Development	1.8	8.6	10.0	20.4	0.4	0.9	0.2	0.4
(12) Visiting Lecturers	6.6	3.3	35.5	45.4	1.3	0.4	0.8	0.8
(13) TOTAL	$501.6	$935.9	$4,344.7	$5,782.2	100.0%	100.0%	100.0%	100.0%

Columns and rows may not add due to rounding.

Source: American Society for Engineering Education

Structure, Part II

The Lead-in

[An appropriate lead-in to the following chart was provided. *Note:* The discussion following the chart focused on the fact that while net income had been relatively flat since 1981, operating profit had grown at an average annual rate of 95.7%. Also discussed, as an aside, was the significant contribution to operating profit of the new product line.]

(Exhibit follows on next page.)

EXHIBIT X
QUIZAMATIC Company
Summary Income Statement
1981–1985

($000)

	(1)	(2)	(3)	(4)	(5)	(6)	(7)	(8)	(9)	(10)
	Net Sales	Cost of Goods Sold	Gross Profit	Operating Expenses	Operating Profit	Operating Profit Contr. by the New Line(a)	Other Income/ (Exp.)(b)	Pretax Income	Taxes	Net Income
(1) 1981	$735	$370	$365	$340	$25	$	$(12)	$13	$(39)(c)	$52
(2) 1982	889	430	459	400	59		(17)	42	(11)(c)	53
(3) 1983	1,234	479	755	640	115	47	(11)	104	47	57
(4) 1984	1,687	678	1,009	780	229	123	(33)	196	121	75
(5) 1985	2,222	835	1,387	1,020	367	248	(93)	274	195	79

(a) The new line of products was not introduced until March of 1983.
(b) Primarily includes interest expense on debt.
(c) Tax loss carryforwards from 1980 were utilized in 1981 and 1982.

Make the appropriate improvements and read Review 4 for the answers.

Structure, Part II

Tiers. Do not be afraid to tier your data. Oftentimes the reader is left hanging because he is given, for example, sales and earnings data from 1981 to 1985 but *not* the average annual growth rates from 1981 to 1985. Such is the case in the Challenge chart. And, since the focus of the discussion is on the growth rate of operating profit compared with the growth rate of net income (neither of which is shown!), this Challenge chart is especially frustrating. These growth rate data should be shown in a second tier directly underneath the primary data. In addition, we recommend a third tier showing percent-of-sales data. The first two columns of the revised Challenge chart (shown in full on page 168) are presented below to illustrate.

		Net Sales	Cost of Goods Sold
(1)	1981	$735	$370
(2)	1982	889	430
	.	.	.
	.	.	.
	.	.	.

	Avg. Ann. % Variance Fav./(Unfav.)		
(6)	1981–1985	31.9%	22.6%

as a Percent of Net Sales

(7)	1981	100.0%	50.3%
(8)	1982	100.0	48.4
	.	.	.
	.	.	.
	.	.	.

Highlighting data. The moral of a story should never be a mystery—it should be both evident and forceful. Similarly, the "moral" of a chart should never be a mystery. Thus, it is important to highlight those few pieces of data that carry the core message of the chart. Highlighting can be accomplished in several ways. With tables, "boxing" is probably the most effective, though arrows can be used also. (Generally, you would box—or point an arrow at—those pieces of information that are referred to in the text or in the oral presentation.) With graphic charts, shading or color differences, as well as boxes and arrows, can be used to highlight key components.

In the Challenge chart, the moral of the story is that while net income has grown at an average annual rate of 11.0% from 1981 to 1985, the operating profit—a better indication of success for the operation—has grown at a 95.7% average annual rate. (*Note:* These average annual rates were obtained from the newly constructed second tier of data.) Thus, it would be appropriate to box each of these numbers and, perhaps, to draw a line from one box to the other for purposes of easy comparison. In addition, it might be appropriate to box the operating-profit-as-a-percent-of-sales data (column 5, third tier), for they show an impressive increase of operating margin from 3.4% in 1981 to 16.5% in 1985. A portion of the revised Challenge chart has been extracted on page 166 to illustrate how highlighting can be effected (and effective).

As an aside, for those of you who worry that adding more tiers means potentially creating more confusion, highlighting allows you to have your cake and eat it, too. You can add more tiers—and thus provide more information for the intellectually curious—while maintaining a focus on the core message of the chart.

Memo columns/rows. Columns or rows that are inserted as "memo" items and that interrupt the ordinary flow of information should be designated as "memo" columns or rows. Column 6 in the Challenge chart serves as an example. It was included to provide additional insightful information (*i.e.,* "no-

(5)	(6) MEMO: Operating Profit Contr. by the New Line(a)	(7) Other Income/ (Exp.)(b)	(8) Pretax Income	(9) Taxes	(10) Net Income
Operating Profit					
$25	$ NA	$(12)	$13	$(39)(c)	$52
59	NA	(17)	42	(11)(c)	53
115	47	(11)	104	47	57
229	123	(33)	196	121	75
367	248	(93)	274	195	79
95.7%	ND%	66.8%	114.3%	ND%	11.0%

tice how much of our operating profit has been contributed by the new line of products!'') but does not ordinarily belong in a summary income statement (for example, while all the other columns are "additive" to the net profit data in column 10, column 6 is not). To correct the situation, simply add the word "memo" to the beginning of the column title, as is shown below.

(6)
MEMO:
Operating
Profit
Contr. by
the New
Line(a)

Avoid blanks. Avoid blank spaces in a chart at all costs. Blank spaces give the appearance of unfinished business. If something is zero (note column 6, rows 1 and 2), don't leave it blank; use "0" or "–" instead. If something is not applicable, not available, not determinable, or not projected, then indicate it using the following guidelines: For internal documents, if your company has standard abbreviations (such as NA, ND, etc.) for these situations, use them. If your company does not have such standard abbreviations, we recommend the list below, to be used in conjunction with a simple legend contained in your chart to explain the abbreviations.

Not Applicable = NA

There may be places in the chart where a piece of data does not apply; "NA" is appropriate in such places. Do consider, however, using a footnote in the place of "NA" if you feel it is important to tell the reader why the data is not applicable.

Not Available = (Footnote)

We suggest using a footnote to indicate that information is not available. A footnote will allow the reader to know why it is not available or when it *will* be available. *Do not use "NA" to mean "not available."*

Not Determinable = ND

Some calculations, like $6 \div 0$ (or anything divided by zero), are simply not mathematically determinable. In addition, if you are dividing a number into an "NA," then it is also not determinable. See Appendices B and C for other calculations that are "ND."

Not Projected = NP

Not Budgeted = NB

Not Forecast = NF

While these notations can be used, the use of footnotes should be considered in their place to explain *why* the data were not projected, budgeted, or forecast.

For documents to be distributed *outside* the company, use either *your* company's standard abbreviations or those suggested

EXHIBIT 4-A
CHALLENGE CHART 4 REVISED

EXHIBIT X
QUIZAMATIC Company
Summary Income Statement
1981–1985
($000)

	(1) Net Sales	(2) Cost of Goods Sold	(3) Gross Profit	(4) Operating Expenses	(5) Operating Profit	(6) MEMO: Operating Profit Contr. by the New Line(a)	(7) Other Income/ (Exp.)(b)	(8) Pretax Income	(9) Taxes	(10) Net Income
(1) 1981	$735	$370	$365	$340	$25	$ NA	$(12)	$13	$(39)(c)	$52
(2) 1982	889	430	459	400	59	NA	(17)	42	(11)(c)	53
(3) 1983	1,234	479	755	640	115	47	(11)	104	47	57
(4) 1984	1,687	678	1,009	780	229	123	(33)	196	121	75
(5) 1985	2,222	835	1,387	1,020	367	248	(93)	274	195	79
Avg. Ann. % Variance Fav./(Unfav.)										
(6) 1981–1985	31.9%	22.6%	39.6%	31.6%	95.7%	ND%	66.8%	114.3%	ND%	11.0%

as a Percent of Net Sales

(7) 1981	100.0%	50.3%	49.7%	46.3%	3.4%	NA%	(1.6)%	1.8%	(5.3)%	0.0%
(8) 1982	100.0	48.4	51.6	45.0	6.6	NA	(1.9)	4.7	(1.2)	0.0
(9) 1983	100.0	38.8	61.2	51.9	9.3	3.8	(0.9)	8.4	3.8	4.6
(10) 1984	100.0	40.2	59.8	46.2	13.6	7.3	(2.0)	11.6	7.2	4.4
(11) 1985	100.0	37.6	62.4	45.9	16.5	11.2	(4.2)	12.3	8.8	3.6

(a) The new line of products was not introduced until March of 1983.
(b) Primarily includes interest expense on debt.
(c) Tax loss carryforwards from 1980 were utilized in 1981 and 1982.

above. In either case, though, be certain to use them in conjunction with a simple legend to explain these abbreviations.

In addition, such relatively standard notations as "1985B" (*i.e.*, 1985 Budget), "1985A" (*i.e.*, 1985 Actual), and "1986F" (*i.e.*, 1986 Forecast) may need to be included in such a legend. Your abbreviations, although familiar to you, may be "nonstandard" to an outsider.

Exhibit 4-A shows Challenge Chart 4 with all the revisions recommended above (again, the lead-in is excluded as it required no changes).

(Exhibit appears on preceding page.)

Making the Calculation

The Lead-in

Exhibit X shows the interest earned/foregone calculation for the years 1981–1985.

(Exhibit follows on next page.)

EXHIBIT X
QUIX Company
Calculation of Interest Earned or Foregone
1981–1985

($000)

	(1) Current Yr.'s Cash Flow(a)	(2) Beg. Cash Balance	(3) Avg. Cash Balance from Current Yr.'s Flow	(4) Total Avg. Cash Balance	(5) Pretax Interest Earned/ (Foregone)	(6) Aftertax Interest Earned/ (Foregone)	(7) Ending Cash Balance
(1) 1981	$(159.1)	$ 0.0	$(79.6)	$(79.6)	$(8.0)	$(4.0)	$(167.1)
(2) 1982	67.5	(167.1)	33.8	(133.4)	(13.3)	(6.9)	(106.5)
(3) 1983	65.0	(106.5)	32.5	(74.0)	(7.4)	(3.8)	(45.4)
(4) 1984	63.2	(45.4)	31.6	(13.8)	(1.4)	(0.7)	17.1
(5) 1985	61.4	17.1	30.7	47.8	4.8	2.5	81.0

(a) Cash flow data obtained from Sources and Applications Statement (column 9) of QUIX Company's 1985 annual report.

Make the appropriate improvements and read Review 5 for the answers.

Making the Calculation

Provide column formulas when the derivation of data is not obvious. When scanning the Challenge chart, you may have had a few questions about the derivation of some of the numbers, a situation that probably made the chart difficult to follow.

Let's see what could have been done to avoid such a situation. In the chart, column 7 (the ending cash balance) is equal to column 2 (the beginning cash balance) plus column 1 (the cash that flows into the balance during the year) plus column 6 (the interest earned on the cash balance during the year). Though this formula makes perfect sense once explained, we certainly would not expect or want the reader to derive the formula himself. To make the formula obvious, the creator of the chart should have used one of the following "formula-showcasing" methods.

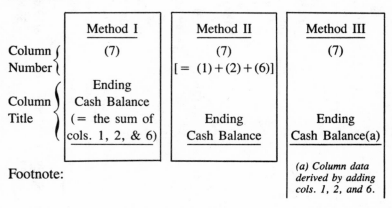

	Method I	Method II	Method III
Column Number	(7)	(7) [= (1) + (2) + (6)]	(7)
Column Title	Ending Cash Balance (= the sum of cols. 1, 2, & 6)	Ending Cash Balance	Ending Cash Balance(a)
Footnote:			*(a) Column data derived by adding cols. 1, 2, and 6.*

(Caution: The footnote option—Method III—can be frustrating for the reader if he has to repeatedly refer to the formula.)

Make assumptions clear. In the Challenge chart it is relatively easy to see that column 5 (pretax interest) is equal to column 4

Exhibit 5-A
CHALLENGE CHART 5 REVISED

EXHIBIT X
QUIX Company
Calculation of Interest Earned or Foregone
1981–1985

($000)

	(1)	(2)	(3)	(4)	(5)	(6)	(7)
			[= 50% of (1)]	[= (2) + (3)]			[= (1) + (2) + (6)]
	Current Yr.'s Cash Flow(a)	Beg. Cash Balance	Avg. Cash Balance from Current Yr.'s Flow	Total Avg. Cash Balance	Pretax Interest Earned/ (Foregone)	Aftertax Interest Earned/ (Foregone)	Ending Cash Balance
(1) 1981	$(159.1)	$ 0.0	$(79.6)	$(79.6)	$(8.0)	$(4.0)	$(163.1)
(2) 1982	67.5	(163.1)	33.8	(129.4)	(12.9)	(6.7)	(102.3)

(3) 1983	65.0	(102.3)	32.5	(69.8)	(7.0)	(3.6)	(41.0)
(4) 1984	63.2	(41.0)	31.6	(9.4)	(0.9)	(0.5)	21.8
(5) 1985	61.4	21.8	30.7	52.5	5.2	2.7	85.9

(a) Cash flow data obtained from Sources and Applications Statement (column 9) of QUIX Company's 1985 annual report.

Assumptions:
(i) Cash generated each year flows evenly throughout the year. Thus, column 3 data represent one-half of column 1 data.
(ii) The interest rate is 10% pretax each year.
(iii) The tax rate is 50% in 1981 and 48% from 1982 to 1985.

(average cash balance) multiplied by an interest rate. By not telling the reader this and by not telling him the exact interest rate used, the chart creator has risked frustrating the reader of the chart. *All important assumptions should be shown.* Below are presented four methods of making assumptions clear.

	Method I	Method II	Method III
Column Number	(5)	(5) [= (4) × 10.0%]	(5)
Column Title	Pretax Interest Earned/ (Foregone) (= col. 4 × 10.0%)	Pretax Interest Earned/ (Foregone)	Pretax Interest Earned/ (Foregone)(a)
Footnote:			*(a) Interest calculated at 10.0%.*
Method IV:	Include an "Assumption" section, listing all important assumptions, below the data section of the chart.		

Check your numbers. Double-check and triple-check the numbers in your chart, time permitting. A reader who finds fault with a *single* number or calculation may lose faith in the entire chart. The credibility of your message is then shaken, if not destroyed.

We certainly didn't expect any reader to check for number accuracy (especially since no formulas or assumptions were provided), but there *is* an error in the chart. The number in row 1, column 7 should be $(163.1) [$(159.1) from column 1 plus $0.0 from column 2 plus $(4.0) from column 6], not $(167.1). Because of this error, all the numbers in column 6 (the *highlighted* column) are wrong, as are several others.

Exhibit 5-A shows Challenge Chart 5 in its revised form, excluding the lead-in.

(Exhibit appears on preceding page.)

Footnotes

The Lead-in

Exhibit X below shows net sales by product line from 1982–1986F.

(Exhibit follows on next page.)

EXHIBIT X
Net Sales by Product Line
1982–1986F

	(1)	(2)	(3)	(4)	(5)	(6)
				Net Sales		
	Industrial Detergents	Multi-Purpose	Linen Supply	Ancillary/Specialty Products	Other(2)	Total
(1) 1982	$ (3)	$ (3)	$ (3)	$ (3)	$ (3)	$27,846
(2) 1983	6,093	8,701	2,663	9,003	3,622	30,082
(3) 1984	7,106	8,349	2,504	8,187	3,464	29,610
(4) 1985B(4)	8,665	9,942	1,929	8,687	3,361	32,584
(5) 1986F(4)	9,456	11,718(1)	2,389	9,810	3,313	36,686

(1) Reflects early field-test results of Multi-Quim. These test results indicate national rollout of the product by June of 1986.

(2) Primarily includes bleaches, starches, and de-wrinkling compounds.

(3) Data for the various product lines are not available for 1982 because products were not classified by product line in the computer until January 1983.

(4) Budget and forecast data provided by management.

Make the appropriate improvements and read Review 6 for the answer.

Footnotes

Footnotes are often mishandled, and thus misunderstood, in charts. The discussion below highlights the important areas in the art of footnoting.

When to use footnotes. Footnotes should be used:

1. to indicate the reason behind unusual trends and variances [footnote (1) in the Challenge chart is an example of this use];
2. to describe what is included in a significant "other" column [see footnote (2)];
3. to explain why information is not available [see footnote (3)];
4. to indicate the source of information [see footnote (4)].

Letters, not numbers. It is the convention to use *numbered* footnotes in the *text* of a document. This makes a great deal of sense, we think, because it would be potentially confusing to use *lettered* footnotes in a sea of other letters. Why, then, would someone use numbered footnotes in a chart, which happens to be a sea of numbers? The Challenge chart, which uses numbered footnotes, looks muddled and risks confusion. We strongly recommend, therefore, that letters (surrounded by parentheses) be used to represent footnotes in a chart.

The order. If you ever get past footnote (z), heaven forbid, the following recommended sequence of footnotes may be helpful.

(a), (b), (c) . . . (z),
(aa), (ab), (ac) . . . (az),
(ba), (bb), (bc) . . . (bz),

.
.
.

(za), (zb), (zc) . . . (zz).

This sequence of footnotes cannot be applied to footnoted material randomly. Rather, the sequence should be applied either on a left-to-right basis (*i.e.,* footnotes (a), (b), and (c) should be applied to footnoted material in the left-most columns of the chart and the last footnote letters should be applied to material in the right-most columns) or on a top-to-bottom basis.

Positions. Each footnote should be positioned immediately to the right of any figures to which the corresponding footnoted material pertains. As for the positioning of the corresponding footnote "text," it can be placed either at the bottom of the chart or to the right of the chart, as long as it is placed *somewhere on the same page as the chart.*

Exhibit 6-A shows Challenge Chart 6 (excluding the lead-in), which has been revised to incorporate the improvements recommended above.

(Exhibit follows on next page.)

EXHIBIT 6-A
CHALLENGE CHART 6 REVISED

EXHIBIT X

New Sales by Product Line
1982–1986F

	(1)	(2)	(3)	(4)	(5)	(6)
				Net Sales		
	Industrial Detergents	Multi-Purpose	Linen Supply	Ancillary/ Specialty Products	Other(a)	Total
(1) 1982	$ (b)	$ (b)	$ (b)	$ (b)	$ (b)	$27,846
(2) 1983	6,093	8,701	2,663	9,003	3,622	30,082
(3) 1984	7,106	8,349	2,504	8,187	3,464	29,610
(4) 1985B(c)	8,665	9,942	1,929	8,687	3,361	32,584
(5) 1986F(c)	9,456	11,718(d)	2,389	9,810	3,313	36,686

(a) Primarily includes bleaches, starches, and de-wrinkling compounds.
(b) Data for the various product lines are not available for 1982 because products were not classified by product line in the computer until January 1983.
(c) Budget and forecast data provided by management.
(d) Reflects early field-test results of Multi-Quim. These test results indicate national rollout of the product by June of 1986.

Graphic Charts

The Lead-in

The chart below depicts our company's sales growth record from 1975 to 1979.

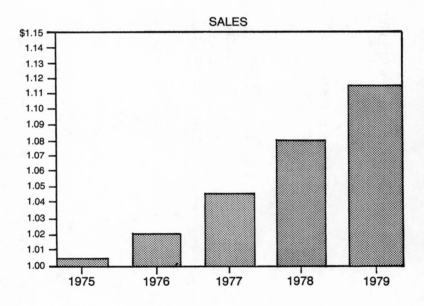

SALES

Make the appropriate improvements and read Review 7 for the answers.

Graphic Charts

Cosmetics. An appropriate title, appropriate headings and source information, and effective highlighting are as important with graphic charts as they are with tabular charts. Concerning the Challenge chart, no source information is provided, no axis "headings" are shown, none of the key data are highlighted (although this is more of an "optional" feature with graphs than with tables), and the title is incomplete. These failings, in combination, result in a poor graphic display.

Eliminate distortions (unless intended, of course). There are three primary ways, using graphics, to distort the appearance of a trend. The most harmless way is to "compress" the horizontal axis, as shown below (both graphs represent the same data):

The Effect of Compressing

GRAPH I

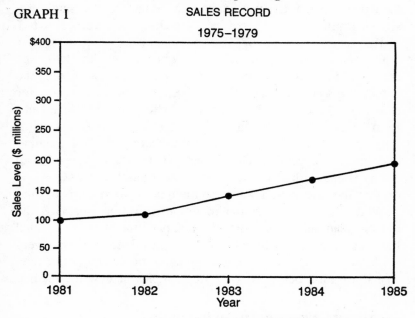

SALES RECORD

1975–1979

GRAPH II

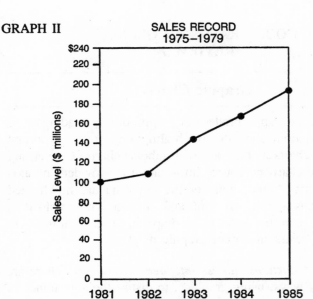

SALES RECORD
1975–1979

As shown above, Graph II implies a much faster growth rate than does Graph I, even though the data are the same. (A similar result can be effected by "stretching" the vertical axis.)

The second method of distortion involves using a number other than zero at the origin (the origin is where the two axes meet). This method is more sinful than the first in that the potential distortion is significant. Take the Challenge chart, for example. The bars in the chart imply excellent growth in sales from 1975 to 1979, but, in reality, the growth averages a paltry 2.6% per year, 5.2% pts. *below* the average rate of inflation over the same period. The disparity between appearance and reality is caused by the use of a non-zero number ($1.00) at the origin. So remember, always use the number zero at the origin.

While the second method of graph distortion is sinful, the third is insidious. This is the "broken bar" method—also called the "cut graph" method—and it is insidious because every book we've read on the subject actually *endorses* the practice. The illustration below shows two examples of how the method works.

How the Broken Bar Method Can Distort Charts

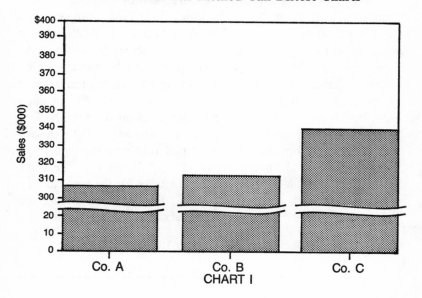

CHART I

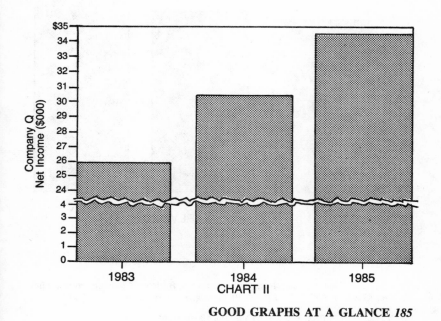

CHART II

Despite having zeroes at the origin, both of these charts still distort the comparability of the data. Note how Company C's sales level appears to be about twice that of B and A; in actuality, Company C is only 10% or so larger than B and A. Similarly, note how Company Q appears to be increasing its earnings rather impressively, when, in reality, earnings have increased at an average annual rate of less than 1%. In each case, the misrepresentation of data can be blamed on the broken bar method. This method is "needed," according to the books that endorse it, because the quantities involved are "so large that the chart would become unwieldy."* Nonsense. The chart would not be unwieldy if appropriate values for the vertical axis were used in each case. To illustrate, the charts below are the revised versions of the ones shown above.

Broken Bar Charts Revised

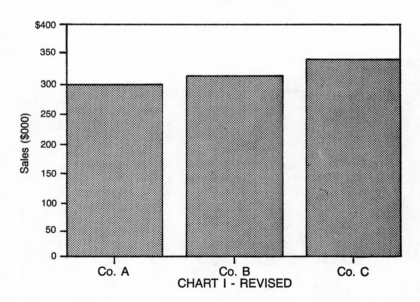

CHART I - REVISED

*Himstreet, William C., and Baty, Wayne Murlin, Business Communications, *Fifth Edition* (Belmont, Calif.: Wadsworth Publishing, Inc., 1977), p. 298.

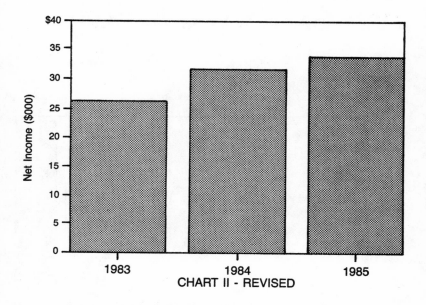

CHART II - REVISED

As shown above, the need to break the bars is eliminated by increasing the gradation range on the vertical axis: In Chart I, it was increased from a range of 10 (from 300 to 310 to 320, etc.) to a range of 50 (from 0 to 50 to 100, etc.); in Chart II, it was increased from a 1-unit range to a 5-unit range. Such revisions give more honest depictions of the data and allow better comparisons.

One exception to the "Don't Use a Broken Bar" rule does exist, however. If one or two bars in a chart are *excessively* longer than the other bars, you might want to break them. But break only those that are excessively longer; and break them at a point that allows the other bars to be shown in full; and break them in such a way that the extreme difference in size between the broken bars and the shorter bars is still evident. The following chart shows an appropriate situation in which to break bars.

The Broken Bar Method Appropriately Applied

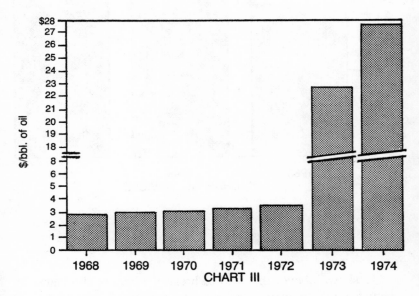

CHART III

Additional information. Do not be afraid to add useful information, where appropriate, to these graphic displays. For example, in the Challenge chart, the average annual growth rate from 1975 to 1979 could (and probably should) be displayed. The right side of the chart would be a convenient place. In addition, the individual bars in the chart could each show the breakdown of sales by division. Do not, however, add information just to add information. Make certain the additional information adds to your purpose.

A revised version of the Challenge chart, incorporating the suggested changes, is shown in Exhibit 7-A (the lead-in is excluded as no corrections were appropriate).

(Exhibit follows on next page.)

EXHIBIT 7-A
CHALLENGE CHART 7 REVISED

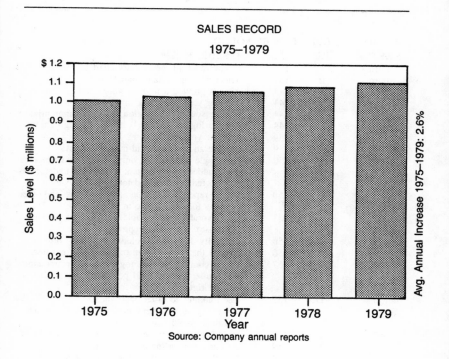

SALES RECORD

1975–1979

Sales Level ($ millions)

Year

Source: Company annual reports

Avg. Annual Increase 1975–1979: 2.6%

GOOD GRAPHS at a GLANCE
SUMMARY

WHERE THE RULE CAN BE FOUND

Challenge	Item	Page	The General Rule
Intro.	A	131	Be aware of all the primary chart forms.
Intro.	B	131	Select the appropriate chart form.
1	A	143	Always provide a title for your chart.
1	B	143	Number your rows and columns.
1	C	144	Include source information whenever appropriate.
1	D	144	Provide logical "breaks" in the spacing of rows.
1	E	144	Number your charts.
2	A	149	Provide an effective lead-in to the chart.
2	B	150	Use single underscores only when a column is being added or subtracted; use double underscores only to indicate a grand total.
2	C	150	Do not repeat dollar signs, percent signs, and other symbols for each figure in a column.
2	D	151	Use favorable/(unfavorable), rather than increase/(decrease), whenever appropriate.
3	A	156	Use fully descriptive column (and row) titles.
3	B	156	Present the total column (or the total row) last.
3	C	157	Group comparable data together (dollar amounts with dollar amounts and percent figures with percent figures).
3	D	157	Use rankings to order data whenever a chronological or other "natural" ordering is not possible. Avoid alphabetical listings.
3	E	158	Include an appropriate number of significant digits.
3	F	159	Be consistent in the use of decimals.
4	A	164	Include second or third tiers when appropriate.
4	B	165	Highlight the key data of a chart.
4	C	166	Include "memo" columns and rows when appropriate.
4	D	167	Avoid blanks in a chart.
5	A	173	Provide column formulas when the derivation of data is not obvious.
5	B	173	Make assumptions clear.
5	C	176	Check your work.
6	A	179	Footnote appropriate material.
6	B	179	Use lettered footnotes, not numbered footnotes, in charts.
6	C	180	Use the appropriate sequence of letters to indicate footnotes.
6	D	180	Correctly position the footnote indicator and the corresponding footnoted material.

Challenge	Item	Page	The General Rule
7	A	183	Include appropriate titles, appropriate headings and source information, and effective highlighting in all graphic charts.
7	B	183	Eliminate distortion in graphic charts: 1. Be "fair" in constructing the axes. 2. Use the number zero at the origin. 3. Use the broken bar method only when appropriate.
7	C	188	Add additional textual or numeric information when it adds to your purpose.

APPENDIX A
MACRO-ECONOMIC DATA

| | (1) Industrial Production Index 1967=100 | Gross National Product | | | (5) Consumer Price Index, All Items 1967=100 | (6) Producer Price Index, All Items 1967=100 |
		(2) Current Dollars	(3) Constant Dollars	(4) Price Deflator		
(1) 1966	97.8	$ 757.5	$ 984.7	76.9	97.2	99.8
(2) 1967	100.0	803.4	1,011.3	79.4	100.0	100.0
(3) 1968	106.3	876.2	1,057.9	82.8	104.2	102.5
(4) 1969	111.1	944.2	1,087.5	86.8	109.8	106.5
(5) 1970	107.8	992.7	1,086.0	91.4	116.3	110.4
(6) 1971	109.6	1,077.6	1,122.0	96.0	121.3	114.0
(7) 1972	119.7	1,185.9	1,185.9	100.0	125.3	119.1
(8) 1973	129.8	1,326.4	1,254.0	105.8	133.1	134.7
(9) 1974	129.3	1,434.2	1,246.0	115.1	147.7	160.1
(10) 1975	117.8	1,549.2	1,232.0	125.7	161.2	174.9
(11) 1976	130.5	1,718.0	1,298.0	132.4	170.5	183.0
(12) 1977	138.2	1,918.3	1,370.0	140.0	181.5	194.2

(13) 1978	146.1	2,163.9	1,439.0	150.4	195.4	209.3
(14) 1979	152.5	2,417.8	1,479.0	163.5	217.4	235.6
(15) 1980	147.0	2,631.7	1,474.0	178.5	246.8	268.8
(16) 1981	151.0	2,954.1	1,513.8	195.1	272.4	293.4
(17) 1982	138.6	3,073.0	1,485.4	206.9	289.1	299.3
(18) 1983	147.6	3,310.5	1,535.3	215.6	298.4	303.1
(19) 1984	163.3	3,658.7	1,637.6	223.4	311.3	310.3

% Increase/(Decrease) Over Prior Year

(20) 1967	2.2 %	6.1%	2.7 %	3.3%	2.9%	0.2%
(21) 1968	6.3	9.1	4.6	4.3	4.2	2.5
(22) 1969	4.5	7.8	2.8	4.8	5.4	3.9
(23) 1970	(3.0)	5.1	(0.1)	5.3	5.9	3.7
(24) 1971	1.7	8.6	3.3	5.1	4.3	3.3
(25) 1972	9.2	10.1	5.7	4.1	3.3	4.5
(26) 1973	8.4	11.8	5.7	5.8	6.2	13.1
(27) 1974	(0.4)	8.1	(0.6)	8.8	11.0	18.9
(28) 1975	(8.9)	8.0	(1.1)	9.2	9.1	9.2
(29) 1976	10.8	10.9	5.4	5.3	5.8	4.6
(30) 1977	5.9	11.7	5.5	5.8	6.5	6.1

(31) 1978	5.7	12.8	5.0	7.4	7.7	7.8
(32) 1979	4.4	11.7	2.8	8.7	11.3	12.6
(33) 1980	(3.6)	8.8	(0.3)	9.2	13.5	14.1
(34) 1981	2.7	12.3	2.7	9.3	10.4	9.2
(35) 1982	(8.2)	4.0	(1.9)	6.0	6.1	2.0
(36) 1983	6.5	7.7	3.4	4.2	3.2	1.3
(37) 1984	10.6	10.5	6.7	3.6	4.3	2.4

Note: For more information on the above data, refer to the following phone numbers:

Industrial Production Index: (202) 452-3154
Gross National Product: (202) 523-0824
Consumer Price Index: (202) 272-5160
Producer Price Index: (202) 272-5113

Also, the *Statistical Abstract of the United States* is an excellent source for any of the above data or for other relevant economic information.

APPENDIX B
CALCULATION OF % VARIANCES

(1) COMPARATIVE AMOUNT (*e.g.*, Actual or Current Year) vs.	(2) BASE AMOUNT (*e.g.*, Budget or Prior Year) =	(3) % Variance: Incr./(Decr.) or Fav./(Unfav.)(a)
(1) Positive or negative	Zero	N.D. %
(2) Zero	Zero	Zero %
(3) Positive	Equal positive	Zero %
(4) Larger positive	Smaller positive	Positive %
e.g., 10	*e.g.*, 5	*e.g.*, 100.0%
(5) Smaller positive	Larger positive	Negative %
e.g., 5	*e.g.*, 10	*e.g.*, (50.0)%
(6) Zero	Positive	(100.0)%
(7) Zero	Negative	100.0%
(8) Negative	Equal negative	Zero %
(9) Larger negative (farther from 0)	Smaller negative (closer to 0)	Negative %
e.g., (15)	*e.g.*, (10)	*e.g.*, (50.0)%
(10) Smaller negative (closer to 0)	Larger negative (farther from 0)	Positive %
e.g., (10)	*e.g.*, (15)	*e.g.*, 33.3%
(11) Positive	Negative	N.D. %
(12) Negative	Positive	Negative %

(a) Variances or percent changes should always explicitly state whether they are expressed on a fav./(unfav.) or an incr./(decr.) basis.

APPENDIX C
CALCULATION OF PERCENT RETURNS

(1) NUMERATOR (Net Income)	(2) DENOMINATOR (Sales or Stockholders' Equity)	(3) RESULT (Return on Sales or on Stockholders' Equity)
(1) Positive, zero, or negative	Zero	N.D. %
(2) Positive	Positive	Positive %
(3) Zero	Positive	Zero %
(4) Negative	Positive	Negative %
(5) Positive, zero, or negative	Negative	N.D. %

INDEX

Active voice *v* passive voice, 114–16
Adjectives. *See* Compound adjectives
"Adverse" *v* "averse," 118, 120
"Affect" *v* "effect," 10–13
"Agenda, agendas," 80
"And." *See also* Conjunctions
  starting a sentence with, 43
Annual reports
  and collective nouns, 83
  credibility and double checking, 121–24
  use of dashes, 102–105
Apostrophes, 92–94
Apportioning nouns, 44–46, 50–53
"As though," and singular noun, 91
"Averse" *v* "adverse," 118, 120

Bar charts (columns), 131, 133–35, 137
  See also Columns
  frequency distribution relationship, 137
  parts of a whole relationship, 135
  for ranking items, 134
  for time series comparison, 133
Bartzke, Rudy, 72
Berger, Stephen, 42
Bernstein, Theodore, 67
"Between you and me" *v* "I," 72–75
Board (of directors), *it* or *they*, 82–83
  subject/verb agreement, 44–45
Brokaw, Tom, 72
"But." *See also* Conjunctions
  starting a sentence with, 42–43

Calculation charts, 171–76
  assumptions clarified, 173–74
  column formulas, 173, 174
  numbers checked, 176
Calculation of Percent Returns, 196
Calculation of % Variances, 195
Careful Writer, The, 67
Chancellor, John, 72, 75
Chart structure, 154–70. *See also* Charts;
  Graphic charts

abbreviations used, 167, 170
and blank spaces, 166
column titles, 156, 157
digits and decimals, 158–59
grouping comparable data, 157
highlighting data, 165–66
ordering of data, 158
tiers, 164
and total column, 156–57
Charts, 127–28, 131–32. *See also* Calculation charts; Chart structure; Graphic charts
favorable/unfavorable variances, 150, 151
footnotes, 177–81
forms for, 130–41
lead-ins, 142–43, 147–49
numbering of, 144–45
row and column numbering, 143–44
rules for presentation, 127–28
source information, 144
spacing, 144
symbols, 150
underscoring, 150
Clauses. *See also* Dependent clauses; Independent clauses; Phrases
and parallelism, 67–71
placement of "however," 87–89
"Clientele," *it* or *they*, 83
Cockburn, Alexander, 20
Collective nouns, 82–83
Colloquial terms, 111
Columns (bar charts), 131, 133–35, 137
  formulas for, 173
  titles for, 156
Commas, 95–98
and parenthetical information, 102–104
"Committee," *it* or *they*, 83
Communication, 149
"Company," *it* or *they*, 82–83
"Comparable," 22
"Compare to" *v* "compare with," 19–22
"Comparison," 22

"Compensation," as subject of sentence, 27–28
Compound adjectives, and hyphens, 107–109
Compound subjects
 "neither . . . nor" construction, 56–58
 and verb agreement, 48–49
Conjunctions
 compound subjects and plural verbs, 47–49
 separation with commas, 97
 single/double and balanced sentence structure, 67–71
Consistency
 in chart numbering, 144–46
 in quantitative sentences, 61–64
Correlation chart (dots), 131, 136
Credibility, 121–24
"Criteria" with plural verb, 80

Dangling prepositions, 39–41
Dashes, 102–105
"Data" with plural verb, 79–80
"Department," it or they, 83
Dependent clauses, and subject/verb agreement, 44–46
"Division," it or they, 83
Dollar amounts
 "fewer" v "less," 14, 15
 and percent variances, 16–18
 real v nominal growth rates, 84–86
Dollar-related words, as subjects, 28–29
Dollars, as figures, with singular verbs, 54–55
Dot chart (XY chart), 136

"Earnings per share" (EPS)
 with plural/singular verb, 30–31
 as subject of sentence, 27–28
"Effect" v "affect," 10–13
"Either . . . or" construction
 and balanced sentence structure, 67–71
 and verb choice, 56–58
EPS. See "Earnings per share"

"Farther" v "further," 117, 119–20
"Fewer" v "less," 14–15
Figures v spelling out of numbers, 61–64
"First" v "firstly," 60
Flow chart forms, 139
Footnotes (to charts), 177–81
Frequency distribution chart form, 137
"Further" v "farther," 117, 119–20

Geographical chart forms, 131, 138
Grace, J. Peter, Jr., 9, 32, 39, 65
Graphic charts, 127–28, 131–32, 182–89
 additional information, 188
 distortions, 183–87
 and titles, 183

Growth rates, 84–86

"He" v "him," 33–35
Heinsohn, Tommy, 72
"However"
 placement of, 87–89
 semicolon use and punctuation, 100–101
Hutton, E. L., 32, 39
Hyphens
 and compound adjectives, 106–109
 as dashes, 102–105

"I" or "me"
 as direct object of preposition, 72–75
 with verb "to be," 32–35
"If," and singular noun, 90–91
"Implied" v "inferred," 117, 120
"Importantly," 59–60
"Income," as subject of sentence, 28
Independent clauses
 parenthetical, 102–105
 and punctuation, 99–101
 "that" v "which," 23–26
Industry position chart form, 141
"Inferred" v "implied," 117, 120
Infinitives, splitting of, 36–38
Inflation, adjusting for, 84–86
"Irregardless" v "regardless," 117, 119

Kraus, Albert L., 65

"Lastly" v "last," 60
Lead-ins, 142–43, 148–49
"Lend" v "loan," 117, 119
"Less" v "fewer," 14–15
Lincoln, President Abraham, 42
Line/curve graphs, 131, 133, 137
"Loan" v "lend," 117, 119

Macro-Economic Data, 192–94
"Management," it or they, 83
"Majority," and choice of verb, 51
Map charts, 131, 138
"Me" or "I"
 as direct object of preposition, 72–75
 with verb "to be," 32–35
"Media" and plural verb, 79–81
Minard, Lawrence, 39
"Most," and choice of verb, 51
Mudd, Roger, 72, 75
"Myself," correct usage, 76–78

"Neither . . . nor" construction, 56–58
"Noise"
 and apportioning nouns, 51
 compound subjects and, 47–49, 56–58
 and prepositional phrases, 44–46
None, "is" v "are," 50–53
"Not any" and choice of verb, 53
"Not one" and choice of verb, 53